If there is one person I know wh[illegible] resilience, it's Andry. Finally we ha[illegible] jam packed with practical and re[illegible] responses to stress and uncertainty [illegible] tone is encouraging and energising. She brings together her expertise and experience as a dynamic coach to provide a valuable and informative guide. Every organisation should get their hands on a copy. This book will change lives and shift perspectives.
Jackee Holder, Coach & Author

I think this book has come at a really opportune time in terms of what we are all facing in the world at the moment and will be a great opportunity for people to stop and reflect on their lives and make positive changes using the techniques in Andry's book. We all need a bit more resilience in life and this book gives great techniques to achieving that goal.
Fiona Evans, HR Director of the Year 2017

Andry comes well out-fitted to provide the attentive reader with a variety of classic, as well as innovative techniques and processes that are bound to enhance the work lives of those of you who choose to practice what Andry preaches.
Joel Edelman, Attorney, Mediator and Author

Resilience is a buzz word but what Andry Anastasis McFarlane does in this very timely book is to make it meaningful for those who are facing the impact of COVID, and those who are facing the reality of a constantly changing and increasingly demanding workplace. She moves resilience beyond being a strategy for survival or a quality available to the heroic, into making REAL RESILIENCE a set of skills that can be developed by all of us. As we emerge into a working world changed by a pandemic, this book is a key resource for developing the adaptability, flexibility and self-care that mark those who are REALLY RESILIENT.
Dr Carole Pemberton, Author of *Resilience: A Practical Guide for Coaches*

This edition published in the UK in 2020

Editorial: Bryony Sutherland
Book design: Caroline Goldsmith

Also available as an eBook

The Really Resilient Guide

ANDRY ANASTASIS McFARLANE

For Ray

Author's Note

This book is not intended to provide healthcare advice, whether medical, psychological or of any other kind, nor to diagnose, prevent, cure or treat any condition. This book is certainly not intended to replace the advice of a physician. If you need expert advice, please consult a competent professional. The author is not a medical professional. The techniques and approaches are for your discussion and consideration.

All statements and viewpoints expressed in this book represent the opinions of the author. They should not be considered scientific or correct conclusions. Although the author strives to provide accurate content, she cannot guarantee that the information in the book is free of errors. In addition, each chapter does not provide full and complete information about each subject, and contains information only up to the date of its original publication. There is no warranty of any kind in this book, neither express, nor implied.

Andry Anastasis McFarlane does not assume any liability to any person or entity in relation to any loss or damage, of whatever nature, directly or indirectly related to this book or its information. If, however, you enjoy this book and find it useful, please write and tell the author on the Amazon/Kindle page.

Contents

Introduction: Why We Need to be More Resilient at Work

- **'There's always so much going on at work. I can't keep going.'**
- **'Change is coming – we need to get the whole team ready – encouraging each other more and being less scared of constructive feedback.'**
- **'I'm not sure how to handle the changing work culture. It's not my cup of tea.'**
- **'I'm worn out – I'm leaving work late after arriving early.'**
- **'I've been through a challenging time – I haven't quite bounced back.'**
- **'Opportunities keep passing me by and I can't understand why.'**
- **'These are disruptive times – but whilst others seem to be embracing and even creating "disruptive change", I'm not feeling so open or innovative.'**
- **'Everything is so uncertain at work – I feel unsettled.'**

The nature of working life has changed radically in the last decade. It's faster, more demanding and more digital. For many, that means it's more enjoyable: for example, the emergence of co-working spaces means small businesses like my own have fantastic new community-focused work environments that may still emerge successfully from lockdown. An increase in people working from home, accelerated by COVID, means for many less travel, less rush-hour chaos and less stress, which can only be beneficial. But undoubtedly you will have also noticed and felt the stressful effects of lockdown, the previous global financial crash and a deep sense of uncertainty in life. This era has even developed a new acronym: VUCA (Volatility, Uncertainty, Complexity and Ambiguity).

Perhaps you've felt like your whole work landscape is changing? During the global financial crisis, many of my workplace coaching clients and workshop clients found that their teams shrank in size. Professional and personal budgets were cut. Huge changes occurred in unexpected ways and seemingly at the speed of light. Afterwards, people adjusted, recovered and found new jobs and new sources of income, developing a mindset of survival and resilience. Many people I spoke with now had more areas of responsibility in the same jobs. Yet they often faced more uncertainty, more adversity and more chaos.

During the COVID and lockdown crisis, many of my clients, neighbours, friends and colleagues immediately lost much of their work and were forced into challenging financial positions. They had to adapt to suddenly having lots of time on their hands. Other clients were working longer hours than usual and dealing with challenges and staff emergencies from home, often in circumstances which were unsuitable as offices.

For younger colleagues at the beginning of their working lives, the temporariness of contracts and constant uncertainty at work over the last few years has been all that they have known: short-term contracts, high staff turnover, loss of clients, sudden changes to working from home, flat structures with no chance of promotion (and no line-manager), disruption-based work cultures, a lack of financial security. After the financial crisis, this eventually led to engagement, innovation and even excitement, but also deep stress.

In the world of learning new workplace skills, 'disruption' as innovation has brought changes to how we learn, such as online learning alongside face-to-face learning. In the commercial world, digital innovation has affected how we shop (easier and even safer online, but a loss for high streets and markets), how we book transport (hire cars by the hour, from the end of your street) and how we use our commute (checking emails or social media as we travel).

In response to these crises and changes, many people have had to be flexible – this is one type of resilience. Some businesses adapted and managed to pivot to online more easily than others. For example, during lockdown, food markets launched delivery services, while face-to-face coaches and mentors transformed their businesses online. As we emerge from lockdown, sparks of innovation, and new creative ways of adapting are being initiated in workplaces, and adaptability is emerging as a feature of this resilience. It is clear that many roles, such as admin and IT, can be as or even more effective when working remotely, although the challenges of isolation and online fatigue have yet to be fully addressed.

Others have tapped into a different kind of resilience – they've had to dig deep, find reserves of determination and inner resources they never knew they had. This kind of resilience is much more like traditional 'hard graft', aka 'getting on with it'.

Finally, I've noticed in myself and my clients an evolved workplace resilience emerging: a combination of a 'surviving and thriving'-type perspective. Some of us have recognised or managed to push for the opportunity to change careers, retrain, retire, or create new businesses and business models for a new landscape. For newcomers to the workplace, we have spoken about how to feel grounded and innovate despite an unstable work environment – again, a mix of surviving and thriving.

Understandably, although we may all be flexible and adaptable to a point, we are, I think, a bit like an elastic band. Sometimes we can stretch, but at other times, if we overstretch or stretch too often, we wear thin. Without due care, cracks can appear in our energy, mood, or behaviours. The elastic snaps. We become inflexible or rigid, exhausted, and are simply unable to recognise the opportunity in any change at work. So, even *with* survival resilience, you need time to rest and recoup your energy and work with others. In the disruptive time of COVID and post COVID, it is evident that to be resilient you also need to attend to your wellbeing and learn to collaborate more effectively with others.

How resilience helps you in your working life

Resilience is about both surviving and thriving. It's the process of being adaptable, flexible, having staying power and self-awareness. It's a mindset and a set of behaviours. Well-being is key – otherwise, how could you keep going? All of these qualities form part of what I call a REALLY RESILIENT skill set.

With a REALLY RESILIENT approach, you can adapt and be both innovative and flexible. You can better recover from workplace adversity and embrace change. You'll certainly be more effective at responding to crisis and uncertainty. You'll be an asset on a project, as you'll have increased staying power. You'll learn to *grow* through something new, scary or challenging. Feeling and being REALLY RESILIENT enables you to keep going when others would give up. Equally, you'll learn to recognise when enough is enough and when to leave a job or project.

The REALLY RESILIENT approach also affects the influence you have, because resilient people often make better, calmer workplace decisions, which come from a deeper intuition and are more likely to have a greater positive impact.

How this book helps you be more resilient at work

I've been writing about building personal resilience for nearly a decade. During this time, I've been on a massive resilience learning curve both personally and professionally through job loss, setting up a successful company, personal health issues, total loss of all my client base due to the financial crisis, and regeneration of my business in a fast-changing financial and uncertain political climate. I've lived, breathed, cried and laughed my way to resilience. I've known resilience as my uncomfortable, challenging and rewarding friend.

Whether you are facing a challenge – such as your favourite line manager leaving – or you are in the middle of a change right now – such as a funding cut, a string of temporary contracts, a whole new systems change, or a tough professional relationship – you'll be sure to find a relevant resilience-building technique you can quickly and easily practise at work or at home.

These techniques work because they are drawn from real-life

experiences. They have been tried and tested over many years. My clients have found them incredibly powerful. The techniques are relevant whether you are employed or self-employed, have just begun working, or have been in work for decades. Some of these approaches have been created by me, or inspired by others I have met and worked with. Many of them have an additional deep evidence base, such as the Five Ways of Well-Being and 'Solutions-Focused'.

As you practise the techniques in this book, you'll find that you:

- Embrace change and innovation more easily – with less resistance and more understanding of how these approaches help you at work
- Become aware of the times when you are feeling less resilient and needing more focus on well-being and attending to that
- Become able to tap into ways to regain your energy reserves so that you can keep going in healthy ways – in the face of obstacles or challenge
- Become more flexible to changing priorities and timelines whilst retaining your own core values
- Have more staying power
- Experience improved workplace relationships
- Have more energy and enthusiasm for your work
- Feel increased well-being at work and in life
- Feel and become more productive
- Find it easier to handle particularly busy times of year – such as when you have multiple deadlines
- Embrace different views at work and learn from them, whilst stating and standing up for your own perspective
- Stick to your guns when appropriate, whatever the pushback
- Enjoy increase energy, as you now learn to care for your well-being

In a nutshell, this book presents the most valuable practical, well thought-out resilience techniques for you at work, whatever sector you work in – corporate, government, charity, public or NGOs.

Why trust in these REALLY RESILIENT techniques?

I run a learning and development company and so I've been coaching managers, leaders and other staff, training and consulting for over twenty years. In my work, I have spoken to hundreds of people about what makes them more resilient at work and in life. We've discussed what enables them to cope, bounce back from adversity and begin to thrive. Through coaching, I've heard and suggested resilience strategies, accompanied people on their resilience-building journey and helped them learn about being flexible, adaptable and determined.

On a personal note, over the last ten years I have survived and thrived thorough pitching and promoting on a regular basis, and trusting that work will come in despite numerous rejections. I've learnt to speak regularly in front of audiences of 700 people (for a whole hour and they love it!). Sometimes it's easy; other times it's incredibly hard. Yet here I am: alive, sane, healthy and happier – looking forward to the 'new', whatever it may be. I've lived and learned resilience in and out of work, and turned crisis into coping and increased inner strength.

Additionally, many of the techniques draw on the models, philosophy and ideas of other evidence based approaches, such as Solutions Focused, Mindfulness and Emotional Intelligence. Over several years of research, I've read, used and been inspired by these approaches. I've seen how they contribute to building people's resilience.

How to get the most from this book

Following a key foundation chapter teaching you the basis of resilience, Chapters 2 to 5 are organised as a journey, moving from self-awareness to self-care, to shaping your mindset, to taking individual action and getting unstuck, and finally to learning resilience through collective action. Each chapter contains:

- A focus on what the resilience problem feels like
- A sense of what you will experience with the new skills you can learn
- Real life stories to help you see how the techniques can help
- REALLY RESILIENT techniques for you to try out (preferably as you read)
- A key summary of tips, so you can see at a glance a summary of the insights and practical steps you can take

These chapters are best approached in order, as they form a sequence. However, if you are in a hurry, you can dip into the chapter that seems the most beneficial for you, then jump to another, out of sequence. At the end you will find a few closing words of REALLY RESILIENT insights to keep you inspired, motivated and relaxed.

Please note it helps if you drop your *expectations* about the resilience results you'll get. These techniques are best carried out with a 'life experiment'[1] mindset: 'I'll experiment and notice what might happen as a result.' I've always found this a tough lesson, but a useful one. A more success-orientated approach – 'I'll read this and then X will be sorted,' will just add another layer of stress to your life, preventing you from relaxing and getting the most from each activity.

You might also find it helpful to use a journal to reflect on and record what you experienced. A few days or weeks later, reflect on any changes that happened over time, or any new thoughts or feelings you notice. In that way, you can track your resilience learning.

The link between resilience and your working life and wider life

Work is part of your life. It is not a separate entity. It is how you spend your days and maybe your nights. Obviously, if you're working in an organisation (or co-working space or client's office space), it's not just what's going on in your role or organisation that impacts on your resilience, but what's going on in your *wider life*. So if things are going well at home, you're healthy and financially stable, you feel more resilient. When you feel truly resilient in your wider life, you often feel you can handle almost anything in life and in work.

On the other hand, if you're being challenged in your wider life, e.g. you're moving house, experiencing poor health, drinking too much alcohol, taking drugs, or if a key relationship is in trouble, these factors may impact on your resilience in your working life. After a small setback at work, it may take a few days to build up. But if there has been a larger setback at work or in your wider life, it may take weeks, months or even years to feel more resilient at work or in life again.

Paradoxically, there are times when crisis at work or otherwise seems to bring out our resilient selves. You discover an inner strength at work *because* you are stretched at home; something falls apart in one area and you find an inner resilience in another.

In my experience, resilience comes and goes. During or after a crisis or stressful time, you may feel fragile, inflexible or totally worn out – the opposite of resilience. In those situations, it's even more important that you attend to both your emotional and psychological well-being (see Chapter 2: Five Ways to Well-Being) and also seek outside support. There is often value in slowing down and taking some small practical resilience steps from Chapter 1: Resilience Foundations and Awareness, and absorbing the stories and techniques of Chapter 3: Changing Mindsets. Taking these small steps to build your well-being can help build your overall resilience, without stretching you too much. Some of the techniques mentioned here are useful outside of work too. I also recommend talking with a coach or counsellor.

Who is responsible for building personal resilience? Individual versus organisational responsibility.

Based on my own experiences, it's fairly clear as humans we can build our own personal resilience. With regular practice, you can feel more mentally resilient and have more staying power. Research also shows that if you use a strong community of people (such as your work team), this helps you adapt to unforeseen challenges and changes.

Having said that, it's important that your employer also provides some resilience basics. In my view, employers should share the personal responsibility towards your resilience (these basics might or might not to be upheld by legislation). Examples include Health and Safety, Duty of Care, mental health and well-being services, anti-discrimination practices, RESPECT and co-creating a good working culture, and good HR partner relationships. If you are self-employed or self-employed and working on a regular basis at a key client's office space, this section may still be relevant for you (and for any staff you work with there).

I'd advise that you reflect on whether your organisation has these in place *before* you begin any practical REALLY RESILIENT work. That way you can make the most of any workplace resources, tap into the support you need and negotiate better for change. You'll also be clearer about whether you are working for a sound employer, or if you are expected to be personally resilient without any additional resources or support from them.

The basics that your organisation could (and should) have in place to support your resilience

Does your organisation:

- Create a culture where relationships are healthy and respectful?
- Aim to introduce change at a manageable pace – giving staff and teams adequate time and support to respond, reflect and innovate?
- Ensure that challenges are not overly stressful?
- Promote and support good health and safety practices? This is a legal requirement in most countries.
- Have employee contracts that are fair and non-discriminatory? This is the opposite of the zero-hour contracts that have become so prevalent.
- Support and promote good equality, diversity and inclusion practices? At a recent talk I attended, a young woman said that racism had previously left her feeling she was 'drowning in the bottom of the pool'. This analogy stayed with me and reminded me of the importance of organisations who take seriously equality and diversity practices. They embed the practices into the everyday fabric of the organisation. They live and breathe them. They are respectful and show that equality matters to them.
- Offer emotional and psychological support for staff when required? From employee assistance programs to counselling, staff benefit from an external person to turn to during stress or when physical health affects their well-being. When I worked in a large Further Education College they had a fantastic well-being scheme that ran alongside the National Health Service, so that you could phone a person at that scheme and get quick access to healthcare services. At the very least, your employer should signpost you to relevant services.

Reflect on these features and if they are in place, great. If there are changes pending to put some of these features in place, that's good too. If not, maybe you are less aware of the available resources and could perhaps consult HR? If there are gaps, you could begin to work on your individual resilience with the awareness that it's often tougher to do that without the background of organisational support. In smaller organisations or smaller start-ups, all or some of these features may exist too. If you are self-employed or if you are working in a client's building on a regular basis, the list may be less relevant. However, having an awareness of whether a client has these resilience features in place or not can be useful information for your client relationship.

Obviously, if your organisation is not supportive, or not legally compliant, you might want to speak with a trusted colleague or external confidant to decide if there is anything you can do to address this, perhaps collectively through a group or union. You could use Chapter 5: Let's All Work Together to support you. Privately, you might consider if this is the right place for you to work. I understand that sometimes there may be no choice and you may feel you have to stay – if so, consult Chapter 3: Changing Mindsets and Chapter 4: Launch and Take Action to review this. Alternatively, if you work in HR, you might want to see if you can help introduce some of the features of these supportive workplace practices into your own workplace.

So that's the context. Let's get to the REALLY RESILIENT foundations.

1: Resilience Foundations and Awareness

- **Are you struggling with challenge, regular change, unforeseen disruption or chaos?**
- **Do you need to learn to handle current organisational system change?**
- **Do you want to embrace change, but you don't quite know how?**
- **Do you want to respond positively to a culture of innovation requests or disruptive action?**
- **Are you 'just too tired'? Every. Single. Day?**
- **Are you finding it hard to listen to others, because you are so tired?**
- **Have you reached your limit and do you feel close to burnout?**
- **Do you feel inflexible or rigid most of the time?**
- **Do you find it hard to take on board constructive feedback?**
- **Have you found it hard to 'bounce back' after a stressful time?**
- **Do you feel increasingly vulnerable?**

If some or all of the above apply, this chapter is for you. The list above comprises signs that you are 'NOT-REALLY RESILIENT' ... yet. During this chapter, you'll review this list so you can assess your resilience. You'll discover what resilience is, and what REALLY

RESILIENT is. You'll visualise the signs of being REALLY RESILIENT so you can mentally get ready to be more resilient in the future in your working life. You'll also explore what you want to be resilient to and tap into your willingness to be resilient. Ultimately, this chapter is all about awareness. In the long run, the following insights will help you make better decisions to support your resilience. This forms the foundation work you need for your resilience-building journey.

What is resilience?

When I've looked at resilience in popular culture, it appears heroic, like climbing Mount Everest against all the odds. For most of us, real-life resilience isn't quite as dramatic. It's the ongoing daily quest to survive and thrive through life's challenges and opportunities. We may not climb actual mountains, but the obstacles we learn to overcome may have felt mountainous at one point.

In my experience resilience is…

A. Keeping going. Having staying power and persistence. It's about digging deep and finding inner reserves of strength at times of challenge, change or stress.

B. Adaptability is 'an ability or willingness to change, in order to suit different conditions.'[2] This is similar to flexibility but includes learning to blend in by adapting behaviours, or perhaps modifying your conversational style to be better heard.

Both flexibility and adaptability include thinking and behaving in ways that may highlight for you another, different point of view. This is your ability to step outside of your viewpoint. Sometimes specific techniques can help, such as relaxation and coaching-style conversations. Other times, something as simple as humour can be a way to change your perspective. Flexibility and adaptability also include being able see opportunity in what seem like disadvantages. I'll group flexibility and adaptability together for most of this book, as they share many overlapping features.

C. Flexibility: Resilience comes from the Latin word, *resiliens*, meaning 'rebound' and 'flexible' – like the stem of a flexible plant. Flexibility includes the quality of 'bending easily without breaking'. It also includes being willing to compromise and 'work round' obstacles.

Resilience is not the 'toughen-up and be a sociopath' type of image fed to us by the media, where some leaders ignore what everyone feels and behave like bullies, leaving blood on the floor with each conversation or action taken. It's also not the same as resistance to change, ongoing inflexibility, inability to take on board feedback, or being 'tough' at all times. Sure, there are times to dig deep and develop a thick skin (having been trolled on social media, I have had this experience), but we also need emotional intelligence: the ability to connect, listen and adapt, hear others' views and assess if it's worth persevering or not.

Previously, resilience was defined as 'bouncing back', but I think this is only half the story. When you bounce back, you are recovering from adversity and returning to your starting point. But if we think of 'bouncing *forward*', it gives you a clearer sense that you carry with you into the future new insights – you're learning from your experiences, for use in your present and future work. With this approach, resilience is also seen as a learning opportunity – a chance to deepen skills, find inner strength, flexibility and adaptability. It is an emotional maturing of a kind.

Finally, resilience is not a static moment, it's a changing dynamic. It comes and goes in deep and direct relation to what is going on in our lives. Sometimes feeling flexible, adaptable and having staying power is a quality that lasts for days or even weeks. Then something unsettling such as illness or moving home causes us to feel temporarily vulnerable, so we need to have the awareness of that phase and of when we will be ready to begin rebuilding our resilience.

REALLY RESILIENT features

I've come to believe that what is missing in most resilience-building processes is:

- Self-awareness – the foundation of resilience
- Well-being – a fundamental resilience quality

Also it seems there is:

- Too much focus on 'positive thinking' as a mindset technique for developing resilience skills. I've tried during my whole adult life, yet never quite mastered the art of positive thinking. I'll keep experimenting, but I thought providing some alternatives would be helpful, such as Possibility Thinking and Solutions-Focused Thinking.
- Too much focus on building resilience *alone* – even if you are advised to 'use your network', far too few people get together with colleagues and collaboratively work to support each other to build personal resilience.

REALLY RESILIENT is a broad approach that incorporates all the features above.

Features of being REALLY RESILIENT

REALLY RESILIENT looks and feels like this at work:

1. Greater self-awareness, including awareness of your current state of resilience to work challenges, uncertainty, 'difficult' people and tough tasks or projects
2. Feeling you can more easily adapt and be flexible in response to changes, uncertainty and unexpected challenges at work or noticing when it's time to compromise and taking steps to do so
3. Learning to be at ease at times of uncertainty, ambiguity or confusion at work *or* finding you can accept changes at work

4. Feeling more resourceful during challenging times, so you can more easily find solutions or having a strong network of good relationships to tap into so you can be more resourceful at challenging times

5. Being aware of the times when you are feeling less resilient and need to put more focus on your well-being and perhaps even retreat into resting

6. Taking time to focus on your well-being and re-energising yourself

7. Knowing when and how to keep going and tapping into your staying power

8. Learning to say no and putting boundaries in place or knowing when it's time to leave a project or work situation and taking that step

These eight features form your REALLY RESILIENT list: a combination of inner resilience and outer resilience. Increasing your awareness of these features is key, as awareness is the first step to change.

With regular practise of the techniques explored within this book, this awareness and ability to tap into your flexibility and staying power will slowly and naturally form part of your new mindset and behaviours.

10 Cities – A resilience flexibility story

This is a story about one type of resilience – flexibility – and how it helped my team with an urgent project.

A few years ago I worked on a project with a client. I was based in London, but connecting with people. A colleague and I had pitched the project months ago to a new innovation client. For a long time the client didn't respond, and time was running out. It was a four-week project and I had just three weeks left before I went to work on a different project. I'd need at least two weeks for my team and my part, leaving my assistant with the two remaining weeks to proofread everything I had completed. The project required a three-person team and my colleague had just moved away, so we would be working virtually for the first time as well.

The evening before our potential start date, the contract was signed. I began the following morning. Ideally, we needed additional planning days, but four weeks was all the team had and I now had just two weeks for my part. The project was to create an immense library of over fifty new resources and workshop plans, with the aim of collaboratively creating change in communities. The library of materials would be used in ten cities, with over fifty change makers, to tackle citywide challenges. I was super excited despite the incredibly tight deadline.

I got in touch with the team members. We cleared the decks and tackled the project with enthusiasm and determination, hitting the ground running. Two weeks ensued of research, calls, writing, shaping content, discussion, reflections and meetings. We all flexed our diaries to find slots for Skype meetings with varying work schedules as my team were also busy with other projects in different organisations. My assistant, who prefers to work methodically, with gaps between proofreading days, also adapted her work style, and copy-edited for fourteen days in a row.

I also stepped up to a bigger project management role than I had planned. More days were needed on the project to get the materials completed. I knew the ideal was for me to support the team during the two weeks of editing, but I was leaving for intensive work. I would be on call twenty-four hours a day and I'd have limited time. So my assistant and team adapted how they worked too. That way they *could ask each other* all the questions they had and my assistant would still have support she needed. I could see that it was all possible, but it was somewhat stressful at such short notice. We had to trust each other deeply – fortunately, that was not hard to do.

Four weeks of working at incredible pace, including nearly a dozen Skype planning meetings, we were done. We had pushed, adapted and shown staying power. We had also gently pushed back on additional work requested by the client, as we knew it wasn't possible in the deadline and budget we had.

We had created a fully edited library of materials that any interested facilitator could use to run a collaboration change course. The team's commitment and ability to flex timings, adapt to a new schedule, clear the decks and persist through the challenges was what made it work. We trusted that we could all do that, and we succeeded. That is an example of resilience in action with a focus on adaptability.

TECHNIQUES

Visualising what REALLY RESILIENT looks like in your working life

Visualising is a powerful way to mentally rehearse what you are aiming for in terms of workplace resilience. By using your imagination and envisioning what life will look like when you are more resilient, you are also telling every part of yourself that you are exploring becoming more resilient. You are informing all the bits of your personality that change is likely to be forthcoming. It's worth noting some people 'see' visualisations in their mind's eye or their imagination, while others 'sense' or 'feel' it. However it works for you, go with that – there is no right way. I've heard visualisation is something all good professional sportspeople do: imagine success through the mental rehearsal of visualisation, before they *create* success. So let's take a moment to tap into 'mental rehearsal'.

> Set up: Find a quiet space at work where you won't be disturbed, or do this away from your workplace environment. Allow about five minutes.
>
> Approach: Don't force the visualising, allow it to happen naturally. You might see it, or feel it or sense it. If you are not yet able to visualise, just read the list asking the question, 'Is it possible that I could imagine myself...?' See how that feels.
>
> Activity: Read through the list of REALLY RESILIENT features above. Imagine yourself having some of these experiences in your working life. Imagine what you would be doing, thinking, feeling and saying if this was happening to you on a daily or weekly basis in your working life. What dœs that look like and feel like? What would you be enjoying? What would other people notice is different about you? Take about five minutes to immerse yourself in this visualisation as fully as possible.
>
> Closing question: As you mentally step out of the visualisation, ask yourself: 'What dœs this resilience visualisation show me? Dœs building my personal resilience seem a useful goal for me to work towards?'

This visualisation also works as an awareness-raising activity, as it reminds you of the key signs of resilience.

Signs of low resilience

Feeling more fragile and inflexible (the opposite of resilience) shows up in many ways, either on a daily basis or intermittently:

1. Facing daily uncertainty and ambiguity, and finding it hard going
2. Feeling exhausted *or* feeling close to burnout *or* finding it harder to recover your physical or emotional energy after a stressful time *or* colleagues telling you that you seem tired / exhausted more often
3. Regularly holding it together whilst you are internally falling apart *or* feeling fine on the surface but sensing you are less strong inside
4. Feeling like you don't laugh or authentically smile much anymore
5. Struggling to embrace change and meet the demands of an innovation culture at work *or* feeling inflexible or rigid *or* finding change and uncertainty at work too unsettling *or* colleagues advising you that you are not facing a change
6. Being regularly emotionally triggered by interaction with one person or a group of people *or* feeling highly sensitive to constructive feedback at work or in life
7. Feeling vulnerable or irritable much of the time
8. Having a heavy workload and being unable to say no *or* wanting to give up on a project because you have run out of steam

For freelancers:

- Struggling to stay resilient to the need to pitch, promote and get turned down for work on a regular basis

For teams:

- Your team doesn't respond well to uncertainty and ambiguity
- Your team doesn't innovate or resists change *or* your team is in denial about an upcoming change
- Your team member(s) can't take constructive feedback
- Your team are slow to learn from customer feedback
- Your team lacks joy, humour and a sense of perspective
- Your team are worn out after putting energy into a big project or change

TECHNIQUES

Raise your awareness of signs of low resilience

This is a reflection opportunity. It raises your awareness in the same way that the visualisation above does.

Set up: You'll need at least ten minutes and a quiet space.

Activity: Read over the signs of low resilience above. Work through the list methodically, asking yourself, 'Is that true of me, my team, or my organisation?' If you like, make notes on your reflections. Alternatively, you can discuss the low resilience list with a colleague. That way you can attend to any blind spots about yourselves – checking to see if your self-assessment is accurate from their perspective.

Perform this review during important times of the year. With time and practise, you'll notice earlier when a few of the feelings, mindsets or behaviours begin to loom on the horizon. That way you'll be able to pause, reflect and takes steps to course-correct.

Vary the activity by focusing on a specific area of work, e.g. a person or project, and choosing and adapting the items from the list that seem relevant. For example, with statement number 1 you could add in 'on this project', so it becomes, 'Facing daily uncertainty and ambiguity *on this project* and finding it hard going'.

TECHNIQUES

Assessing your resilience

You can assess your resilience level using different approaches. (For example, Dr Carole Pemberton has a good questionnaire for assessing your resilience in wider life.[3])

Using the Features of Being REALLY RESILIENT and the 'low resilience' list …

> Set up: It's nice to do this seated and relaxed and somewhere quiet. You need ten to twenty minutes.
>
> Activity: Pick a time period to assess, e.g. right now, the last three months, six months or the last year. Read through both lists, seeing if the features are true for you in your working life. When you have gone through both lists, ask yourself, 'Does it seem as if I am resilient at the moment?' You could scale it if you like, from 'very resilient', 'quite resilient', 'a bit resilient' and 'low resilience' to 'not resilient at all'.

You could also have categories comparing your working life with your wider life, and you could keep it evidence based, e.g. I feel am 'very resilient' at work. Evidence: I reacted well to the news of the project funding being cut.

Finally, with time and reflection, you could also connect areas of life and their impact on resilience, exploring if challenges in wider life are affecting resilience at work. E.g. I feel 'a bit resilient' at work and 'quite resilient' in my wider life, as I have recently enjoyed a lovely time socially, but there are huge changes at work that I'm adjusting to. This last bit would be easier to do in conversation with a coach, who might help you to pinpoint any blind spots – we all have them.

Being resilient to things, events and people

I often ask my workshop participants what they would like to be resilient to, and some common themes always crop up. Some of these are cyclical, others are irregular, some expected and others truly unexpected. Some of the common themes are related to systems (such as IT breakdowns) and processes (such as planning templates and learner-documents). Most often, people would like to be more resilient to other people.

Common themes to which people would like a greater resilience:

- Challenging behaviour from team members, line mangers or direct reports
- Policy and processes: Considerable change in policy or practice that affects work, and with which you need to be engaged
- Contracts and regularity: Short contracts, lack of long-term job options, lack of promotion opportunities, irregular work cycle, competition
- People: Change in types of customers or their expectations
- Income changes: Lessening of income, uncertainty of income
- Unexpected financial change: Change in budgets and funding
- Systems change: Restructuring of your organisation, including being on the receiving end
- Task/time pressures: The pace of work and the sheer amount
- Disappointment: Not fully achieving outcomes on projects and programmes
- Pressure: Ongoing and urgent need for innovation and improvement
- Crisis or the unexpected, and the contagious sense of doom and gloom that can pervade individuals and teams

Choosing to be resilient

To some extent I think we choose, through unexpected adversity and challenging times at work, whether we are *willing* to be resilient. We are allowed to simply give up – there's no judgement there. It's not a competition. It's a learning journey; a life experience.

Of course, there are many occasions when there's no choice but to keep going, or to keep being adaptable. However, I've noticed that when I'm having particularly challenging resilience-building experiences at work – such as constantly working late over a long period of time – it helps if I pause and *tap into my willingness*. The answer often gives me renewed energy.

TECHNIQUES

Am I willing to be resilient?

Set up: You can do this anywhere but if you are in a computer-based role, it's good to step away from your screen for a few minutes and be somewhere where you won't be interrupted.

Activity: Bring to mind a workplace challenge and asking yourself the question, 'Am I willing to be more resilient in relation to this?' (You can replace the word 'resilient' with 'adaptable', 'flexible' or 'determined' as necessary.) Replying to your question with a full answer, rather than a simple 'yes' or 'no' can really help you sense your readiness or not. For example:

- 'Yes, I am willing to be resilient.'
- 'No, I'm not yet willing to be resilient.'
- 'I'm not sure if I'm willing to be resilient.'
- If your answer is a yes, allow that to bolster you. If it's a no, or not sure, spend a bit more time investigating and exploring – asking yourself 'why' and 'what would help me feel more willing?'

TECHNIQUES

What do you want to be resilient to?

Set up: Grab a notebook and pen

Activity: Complete the sentence (or discuss with a colleague or someone in your co-working space)

'At work, I want to be resilient to...'

Use the list above to help you get started. Aim to end up with one to three areas. Make it specific.

a ____

b ____

c ____

Now you know more about what you are aiming for, or at least what you want to learn to handle better.

Awareness: the fundamental skill

As you can see, we have been focusing on your *awareness* of signs of resilience. Awareness is one of the most fundamental skills you can have in building your personal resilience. Without awareness, you can't assess how resilient you are with any certainty. You can't have a sense of what you're feeling or thinking; you can't laugh at yourself. Without resilience awareness and emotional awareness, you may also find it hard to connect and engage with other people. You may find yourself in disagreements or having the feeling that things aren't going your way work-wise. And finally, a lack of awareness means it's hard to effect change. Awareness is one of the fundamental emotional intelligence skills outlined by Daniel Goleman[4]. So don't skip this chapter. Let's work on your awareness.

By working on your emotional awareness and consistently practising the techniques and the tips here, you'll become more aware of what you're thinking and feeling, as well as how you're behaving. With awareness, you'll feel like you can understand more what's going on in workplace relationships. You'll be able to read social and work situations more easily. You'll be calmer and more flexible. Awareness comes before conscious action, so your actions will be more thoughtful and therefore could have a better impact. Emotional awareness and resilience awareness is a fundamental mindfulness practice – you'll learn more about this in Chapter 3: Changing Mindsets.

Finally, with a deeper sense of awareness, you're more likely to see opportunities as they arise and will be able to make the most of them.

An awareness resilience story

Years ago, I had an excellent awareness-related, resilience-building experience. A colleague had offered me a job. He was a great negotiator, while I was unskilled in that department (I'm a bit better now!). I was seriously considering his job offer, and wondering if it would suit me. However, there was a degree of discomfort in my feelings that I couldn't place my finger on.

I spoke with my coach. She asked me: 'What do you feel and think?' It quickly became apparent that my gut instinct was working with this person would be difficult. He was great as a freelance colleague, but as a line manager, it wouldn't really work for me – a person who savours her freedom and struggles to hand over her schedule to others.

Through the conversation with my coach, I become aware of my decision. No more negotiating. I decided there and then to continue building my freelance working life, and not to fall back on choosing a job that in the long run wouldn't suit me at all. Awareness in this case was a powerful decision-making aide.

TECHNIQUES

Being present

This is a technique to raise your awareness of your present moment feelings, thoughts and sensations.

Set up: To help you with this, aim to be 'curious', not deciding in advance what you will discover in this activity. Be open to experiencing your thoughts and feelings in the moment. You might feel joyful, neutral or some discomfort. See if you can allow any physical and emotional sensations to be there without trying to fix them.

Activity: Take a few moments away from other people and your computer. Find a quiet space with no distractions. Sit if you can. Take a few slower *breaths* in and out, following the breathing with your mind. Begin to notice your thoughts, then your emotions and then any bodily sensations – if you are hot, cold, tense or relaxed. You might feel joyful, neutral or some discomfort. See if you can allow any physical and emotional sensations to be there without trying to fix them.

Sounds strange? You could notice what you are thinking and feeling right now. (We often get stressed about the future, or worry about the past. So you might notice this too.) You could notice your mood or your feelings – are you sad, worried, flat, depressed? You could also notice how your body feels – tense, relaxed, etc. And then take a gentle breath and see if you can allow a little bit more relaxation.

Sitting calmly, pay attention to *this moment* – to all the *sensory experiences*. Pay attention to the temperature, your breath, any sounds, colours, anything you can smell and hear. Then look around, take it all in, become more aware, see it with fresh eyes – get in the present. Breathe and relax and notice. Stay in this space for a few minutes, breathing and relaxing and noticing.

Over time with practice of being present, you might lower your stress levels and therefore become more resilient.

Awareness and learning

I've been leading professional development workshops in topics ranging from mentoring skills to conflict resolution for more than twenty-five years. When I'm facilitating, I find I work best when I take breaks, but I used to easily run over and break times were consistently late. Somehow I'd slip up on the areas of well-being and organisation. On those less organised days, I ended up speaking faster, asking less questions and being less interactive with participants.

Over the years, what I've noticed is that when I tap into the present moment, I become aware of:

- what I'm feeling (hungry, low on energy)
- what I'm thinking ('I'm a bit stressed', 'I need space' and 'I need a break and perhaps others do too')

I then slow down. I remember to take breaks, ask the participants if it's time for a break, and create more space for participants' questions. I've become more openminded and begun to enjoy myself. All these changes in my experience have led me from being an okay facilitator to being a good facilitator (the feedback from clients has helped me assess this successfully).

In addition, this new way of being present has made me more resilient to demanding training work. There is sometimes a pushback from participants on workshops: 'Our team won't change', 'What's the point of this', 'It's not working' and so on. It's part of the learning curve and it's human and useful. But pushback sometimes takes energy to deal with as a facilitator; I need to remain fully open to supporting someone through their discomfort towards the change they say they want. Awareness helps me take breaks, helps me maintain energy and helps me be more resilient.

Tips: Resilience Foundations and Awareness

- Visualise ideas from the REALLY RESILIENT list
- Reflect on the NOT REALLY RESILIENT list and determine where you fit
- Identify what you want to be resilient to
- Develop awareness of your feelings, thoughts and your sensory awareness on a regular basis, using the being present activity.

2: Five Ways to Well-Being[5]

- **'I've run out of steam.'**
- **'I'm so exhausted that I can't keep going.'**
- **'I feel run down.'**
- **'I'm not enjoying work or life.'**
- **'I no longer do the things that helped me stay fit and relaxed.'**
- **'I never get time to stop for lunch.'**
- **'I can't recall the last time I stopped for a normal friendly conversation.'**
- **'I don't need well-being – I've been doing okay for years. But I also feel unhappy, unfit and unhealthy.'**

How well-being and resilience are linked

I've been researching well-being for twenty-five years and more recently, coaching well-being at work. I lead keynote speeches on how I've used the Five Ways of Well-Being and also 'How to Create a Well-Being Culture'. This has led me to believe that paying attention to your mental and physical well-being is such a major part of being REALLY RESILIENT that I can't overstate it. Perhaps other resilience approaches highlight determination or adaptability, but in my experience, when you are feeling well, your foundation for resilience can be enhanced; it's easier to tap into. You might:

- feel energised enough to have more staying power

- feel calm enough to be willing to be flexible or compromise
- feel refreshed enough to adapt in the moment to a new situation

Paradoxically, often when we are ill and consciously take care of our well-being, we sometimes uncover sources of resilience we never thought we had. (This may be tied into research that shows that resilience builds under pressure). Being REALLY RESILIENT includes noticing when you need to rest and not keep going – to recoup your energy, so you can be persistent later down the line.

What is well-being at work?

Well-being means two things: feeling good in your mind, body, emotions and spirit; and flourishing in life and work. This might look like:

- Feeling healthier
- Having more energy to carry out your activities
- Enjoying your work and feeling inspired
- Feeling proud of the results you're achieving
- Having a satisfying career
- Experiencing 'healthy, motivating' stress (as opposed to chronic, debilitating stress)
- Having a sense of both fitness and relaxation in your body
- Having enough time to stop for lunch and breaks
- Arriving and leaving on time and not regularly working additional overtime due to a heavy workload
- Having time to connect with colleagues and have normal, everyday conversations that are not stressful

When you have well-being, because you have more energy, calmness and inner strength, it's sometimes easier to tap into resilience: to experience it; to tap into being flexible, adaptable and determined. Most people scale their well-being from being unhappy and not getting anything valuable out of working life to being happy and satisfied, and flourishing. They might also add to that 'feeling healthy', putting the two together as 'health and well-being'.

Media messages and well-being

The media would have us believe well-being is going to be an expensive, demanding or confusing business. There are multiple contradictory messages about how to create well-being. Here are some examples I have seen in online newspapers and magazines:

- You could go travelling: 'Is this the fittest hotel in the world?' – *Evening Standard*[6]
- Laugh at yourself: 'Self-deprecating humour linked to greater psychological well-being' – *The Independent*[7]
- Get outdoors: 'Scientists Have Worked Out The Optimal Dose Of Nature Required For Health And Well-being' – *Forbes Magazine*[8]
- Support someone: 'I started mentoring young people and gave my own life purpose' – *The Guardian*[9]

When I researched the 'Five Ways to Well-Being', I discovered that they are evidence-based, intuitive and mostly free. They are also easy to carry out. We now know with innovations such as neuroscience that it is possible to change the habits of a lifetime. So if you think 'I'll never manage to learn to care for my well-being', rest reassured not only does your brain plasticity show that you can learn habits long into your life, but also here I am offering you five easy, intuitive ways to enhance your well-being.

The original aim of the Five Ways of Well-Being was to identify simple, universal actions that anyone can do on an individual level, to improve their mental well-being. These methods were developed by New Economics Foundation, in a team led by (or including) Nic Marks[10], and are based on evidence gathered in the UK government's 2008 Foresight Project on Mental Capital and Well-Being, including regular European-wide questionnaires from over 20,000 people. More recently, the surveys have begun to examine how regularly the Five Ways of Well-Being are used and the impact they have on individuals' lives. They are also so relevant to our workplaces and to building resilience.

The Five Ways are: **Connect**, Keep **Learning**, Be **Active**, Take **Notice** and **Give**, or CLANG! Let's explore them together.

C: CONNECT – 'Talk and listen. Be there. Feel connected.'[11]

We are definitely social animals. Evidence shows that good relationships – with family, friends, colleagues and our wider communities – are important for our mental well-being. We are generally born of a connection between two humans – even if conceived in a lab, that's still a chemical connection. Evidence shows that building a web of strong connections helps you survive and flourish through challenge and change.

Connecting: Making Uncovered

A few years ago I noticed I was really busy with work, but felt disconnected from my community.

A flyer came through the door advertising a collective of Makers – an organisation who help people making stuff for a hobby to become entrepreneurs. The flyer said they were looking for volunteers. Thus I began my journey with Makerhood[12], a makers' collective supporting hobbyists who want to earn from making cakes, furniture, jewellery and other artwork.

The first event I worked on for Makerhood was helping to coordinate Making Uncovered, a day where every member would set up a small version of their studio/ warehouse space. Members of the public would be able to come along and see what the making process looked like, and sometimes take part in it, for example, having a go at making green wood furniture, screen printing or making skincare products. I was part of a core organising team of six, a wider facilitation team of twenty and a film team of five, along with others organising the café and space. I led on anything related to workshops and liaised with the venue: we had twenty makers with varying needs. Fortunately, we had an adaptable venue manager.

And so, for four to ten hours a week I joined meetings, called facilitators and planned. I was beginning to feel *connected*; I was in the centre of something big and I knew it. I was talking and listening all the time. I was enjoying conversations. The conversations were leading to change and, as I and others listened, we not just listening in a shallow sense – we were being present, really connecting.

When the Making Uncovered day arrived, it attracted over 600 people from all over London – 400 more than we had originally hoped for. It was an outstanding success: twenty-five workshops, a non-commercial feel, many opportunities for people to take part, a pop-up choir, a pop-up café and even a profit for future events made from the on the door donations. People of all ages attended, from eight to eighty. The event led to a film[13] and continued to support makers in creating a business from their hobbies. The event was the highlight of the year for me, leaving me with a feeling of euphoria for months to come. That reinforces the evidence that generosity helps us to feel good, long after the event.

Connecting can also lead to lasting relationships – not just momentary ones. I retained a core group of three friends from that voluntary role: three people I can chat to about almost anything, with whom I go out and share social times.

You don't have to be an extrovert to connect. It can be one other person you are connecting with or many. At work, staring at your screen all day, missing lunch regularly or behaving as if you're too busy to talk can all contribute to having less time to connect with colleagues. Less time to listen. Less time to talk about what really matters. Less time to come up with collaborative approaches to challenges. Email is great, but you can't beat a good face-to-face conversation for reconnecting with colleagues.

Simple conversations that involve listening and sharing can be a much-needed way to find a moment of space and calm. They also remind you how much you are all part of a team, hopefully going in the same direction. For me, as I have a virtual team, those mini conversations with colleagues in our co-working space are one of the wonderful gifts of working life.

TECHNIQUES

Connecting at work

Why not try:

- Mini breaks away from your desk and screen
- Attending a social event so that you can get together and have a laugh away from daily tasks
- Giving a more honest answer when asked 'How are you?'
- Going for lunch with colleagues more often
- Starting a new hobby (mine are mosaics and films)
- Reflecting on and writing about whom in your life you have connected with that has made you feel good or more fulfilled

The benefits of connecting are numerous: better relationships, enjoying your working life more and having the sense that you are not alone with your workplace challenges.

L: Keep LEARNING – 'Embrace new experiences. See opportunities. Surprise yourself.'[14]

Research shows us that adults taking part in part-time learning experience an increase in well-being. They feel healthier, seem to lead healthier lifestyles and even build new social networks.[15] Learning takes you to places you could never previously imagine; at its best it also connects you with others.

Neuroscience shows us that much of the day we run on automatic. Reinforcing the same old neural pathways; old habits of thinking that are efficient to use. To change our habits and to keep ourselves healthy, it is recommended to experiment by learning to *do things differently*, e.g. taking a different route to work. Doing this reminds us that we can learn.[16] To stay mentally in tip-top condition, I have often experimented with:

- Writing with my right hand (I'm left-handed)
- Getting (un)dressed in a totally different way – different order, or socks first/last, etc
- Going to work via different routes
- Brushing my teeth right-handed

From cynical to positive and joyful through learning

A few years ago after a long and difficult time in my personal life, I hit a real low. I was struggling to stay positive. Despite some good projects, I was feeling cynical about work and life in general, and about the state of the world. I thought: 'It's too hard to keep going pitching at work', 'I feel isolated even though I have great clients and a co-working group around me', 'I feel that in this economic climate, work is going nowhere'. Basically a doom and gloom outlook, with added exhaustion. You wouldn't have guessed it to look at me – I'm good at keeping it inside. Still, it was all there under the surface. As a result, I was seeing challenges as obstacles and goals as hard work.

A colleague sent me a request to co-deliver a course with her. It was not something I felt confident to do, as I didn't know the content, so I turned it down. But I did accept her offer to attend the course as a participant.

It was based on a fantastic online course focussing on community and collaborative change. At the first session, I found myself emotionally moved – both positively and negatively. There was a buzz in the room and I felt something interesting was happening here – the beginning of synergy. As the workshops progressed, I enjoyed it more and more. I was learning so much and I was learning every day by reading and watching videos in between sessions. Gradually, I noticed I was beginning to care about life and work again. It was a real turning point in my well-being. (The course later led to one of the best projects of my working year – see Chapter 5: Let's All Work Together.)

TECHNIQUES

Keep Learning

a. At work or in your co-working space, there may be opportunities to take part in Continuing Professional Development (CPD) courses and workshops.

b. Consider: What is it that you're curious to learn that's relevant to your work? Enrol on a course outside of work. Many adult learning colleges allow you to attend one class before committing.

c. If you are a manager, you could explore how you create a learning culture and give permission for learning and learning from mistakes. This allows your staff and therefore talent to develop.

d. Reflect and write about: What am I interested in learning next?

If you are a manager, you could explore how you create a learning culture and give permission for learning and learning from mistakes. This allows your staff and therefore talent to develop.

A: Be ACTIVE – 'Do what you can. Enjoy what you do. Move your mood.'[17]

Findings reveal that individuals who are more physically active are happier. Further, individuals are happier in the moments when they are more physically active.[18]

Move your body, change your emotions

Unlike thoughts in your head, emotions are experienced in your body. Emotions are the response to a thought, e.g. 'My workload with this person is unreasonable' or 'I'm working on a boring project' provoke an emotional response: worry, anger, irritation.

Cognitive Behavioural Therapy (CBT) teaches us that we can change our emotions by being curious about stressful thoughts and re-examining them, asking 'Is it absolutely true?' In addition, there is a larger body of evidence showing that we now know you can change your mood by moving your body.[19]

In my experience, being active can help you feel both physically and emotionally resilient. As an added benefit, walking and other movement opens up the free flow of ideas – thus helping you to solve challenges – another resilience-related area. Some organisations I work with have instigated 'walking meetings', which is a great way to get your creative juices going and stay healthy.

Activity versus exercise

In the Five Ways approach, 'activity' covers both activity and exercise. Activity in my experience ranges from taking a short walk at lunchtime to having a stretch for a few minutes away from your desk or, if you drive a lot for work, stretching between drives. Desk yoga has become popular over the last ten years. My experience is that the more activity you do, the less stressed you are. Especially if you do it in a positive way, where you are beginning to enjoy it.

Noticing the need for activity

This spring it was my forty-ninth birthday. A big event, and one year to go before the big 5-0. Around that time, I noticed my favourite clothes were no longer fitting me. My favourite urban trousers seemed too tight. What was going on? I'd always been a slim woman, but suddenly either the setting on the washing machine was too hot and my clothes had shrunk, or I was putting on weight. Not a problem, I thought. I'm getting older; it's natural. But then I began to notice I was tired too – not energised and feeling a bit foggy in my mind, wanting a nap after lunch. I was exhausted by the end of each day. In retrospect, it may have also been useful to consult my GP, and I recommend you do that if you have similar symptoms.[20]

I looked around. My bike showed signs of rust; I had been catching the bus for my twenty-minute daily walk into my office and back. I had been skipping my stretching routine (every other day for twenty minutes). In a nutshell, my activity was low. Sometimes I'd often miss walking because I was rushing – brushing my teeth with my electric brush as I marched down the road to the bus stop, just so that I could be in on time.

So I decided to start making some changes. Leaving home five minutes earlier so I could have the time to walk into town. Monitoring my steps on my phone and walking home via the park – it might take minutes longer, but it's a lovely, refreshing walk.

It's early days, but I'm noticing a difference: my mood is better, I feel better, more energised and flexible, gradually more able to manage stress. I feel happier and more present. It's the relationship between activity, movement and being alive that this brings to mind. My next steps will be more aerobic exercise, getting back to cycling.

Blue Zones®[21]

Blue Zones® are global communities where people routinely live to be ninety and are healthy. I recall reading research conducted on one of the zones in the Mediterranean. The finding was that people did not sit for more than forty-five-minute periods at a desk or table (or in any one position) during the day. At work, it's vital to notice if you need activity, especially if your job is quite sedentary. I have noticed from being more active through Pilates sessions, that posture begins in the feet, the toes and the heel – not just the spine. That's great for me to remember, even when sitting. I also notice that if I step away from my desk more often, I feel more relaxed and at ease in my body and moods.

TECHNIQUES

Be active

Begin to notice the times that you get more tense in your body. Is it related to being in one position for a long time? Explore how you could incorporate increased activity into your day. Perhaps a particular regular meeting is stressful as it's long and there's a tense atmosphere. Given that you know how you respond to this meeting, you might take a short walk a few minutes beforehand. During the meeting you might try consciously relaxing your body, sitting back in your chair and giving yourself a kind, gentle half-smile that softens the muscles in your whole body. After the meeting, go for another quick walk – just a few minutes to stretch your legs and take a few full breaths before you return to your desk.

Moments you could be active at work

Review your work diary and see where you could add in some activity or exercise time. Outside of work, you could self-assess your mobility, then take part in a suitable activity: dog-walking, running, swimming etc. Choose something that you feel will be enjoyable.

Reflect and write: What has your activity level been like lately?

N: Take NOTICE – 'Appreciate the little things. Savour the moment.'[22]

There are two areas I will discuss with you:

- Noticing what brings you happiness and cultivating a sense of appreciation
- Noticing your surroundings

(For 'noticing yourself' – body, feelings, thoughts – see Chapter 1: Resilience Foundations and Awareness).

What brings you happiness? Gratitude and resilience.

Gratitude and appreciation is part of a mindset and also guides and inspires actions. Gratitude is shown to increase well-being and because of this, in my view, it also adds to your resilience.

I recently met an amazing man who gave me permission to share his story of personal resilience and well-being. He was a security guard and had previously served in the forces. He developed Post-Traumatic Stress Disorder (PTSD). This was his first week back at work in a new job. He described how his mental health sponsor had encouraged him to focus on gratitude, by writing ten things each day that gave him happiness. He told me how this activity and having other new supportive relationships were the most significant things that were helping him manage each day. Although he still had down days, he described a general improvement of feeling better every day.

Research around appreciation and what gives you joy

There has been a great deal of research on mindfulness and well-being to support similar sorts of experiences. Two psychologists from University of Miami and University of California[23] researched gratitude extensively. In one study, participants were asked to write a few sentences each week, focusing on particular topics:

- One group wrote about things that they were grateful for

- A second group wrote about things that had displeased them or irritated them
- A third group wrote about more neutral events that had affected them (with no focus on the events being positive or negative)

Can you guess what happened after ten weeks? The group that wrote about gratitude felt better and more optimistic about their lives. They were better at carrying out goals. Surprisingly, they also exercised more and had fewer visits to healthcare practitioners than those who focused on sources of irritation.

My story: Savour the moment

I would say 'Take Notice' is the hardest area for me. I have found one of the best ways for me to savour the moment is to catch the moments of sunshine. I am a sun worshiper – it's in my Mediterranean genes. Having been born and raised in the UK, I've learnt to savour the rare sunny days. Years ago, during one summer when I felt low, there seemed to be very few splashes of sunshine. I was complaining and moaning and even dreaming at night of my favourite Greek beach.

But then, that same summer, rather than begrudge what I didn't have, I learnt to appreciate the small moments of daily sunshine when they occurred. My mindset became, 'I make the most of each sunny day'. I took myself down to my local lido and soaked up the sun. I felt instantly happier and stronger, and the beach dreams stopped. In this way, I found a new appreciation for life and for each day. I think all of this contributed to me feeling more flexible about the UK summer, and not being in desperate need of a holiday to warmer climes each year.

Nowadays, if I'm working at home, I'll sometimes find five to ten minutes to sit with my laptop in the garden in the one tiny spot that gives me sun on my face. Sometimes, that is all my schedule allows. So I make the most of it. These are the little things to savour.

Of course, the big things to savour alongside cherished family members and friends are those great personal achievements and milestones. Two years ago, I took part in a global live stream discussion. I understood that between 10 and 12,000 people were watching worldwide, as it was screened live to all the course participants who were online. My co-working team and other co-working spaces and I were presenting: it was an incredible buzz. Being present in the moment, I enjoyed it as it was happening, and afterwards I often recall that time with gratitude. These are the bigger moments to savour.

TECHNIQUES

Finding moments to savour inside and outside of work

a. Consider the pleasure of lying in bed for an extra thirty minutes. Or reading a book by one of your favourite authors. Or having a laugh with a colleague as you discuss a piece of work. These are all the moments to notice. Next time you are doing any one of these – or any of your other favourite activities – make a conscious effort to be in the moment and savour the experience.

b. I really love coaching. It's such a privilege to be in a one-to-one conversation with someone who is sharing the story of their goals, their challenges, or obstacles and still has the courage to find out how to keep going. In the deep listening that happens, I see the transformation that takes place. It's that moment I really notice and savour. Is there a conversation you could savour at work? In the next enjoyable work conversation, practise pausing and savouring the moment. Be present and enjoy yourself, enjoy the topic, enjoy the interaction and the ease of it.

c. Noticing others progress: If you are a manager or a company director, aim to notice the good work of your staff. Remember to give to give them feedback, to let them know something's been successful and appreciated. My co-facilitator, Miranda, says I have 'high standards and give high support'. You too could notice when your staff have stepped up to a challenge. Maybe even express what a great pleasure it's been seeing them grow and learn.

Noticing surroundings in nature

This spring, I decided to do something new and so I purchased membership of Kew Gardens. It costs £70 a year and you can visit the gardens as many times as you like during that year. As Kew Gardens has 326 acres and 28,000 living plants, I thought that would be enough for me. I decided to go each week for anywhere between fifteen minutes and two hours. Sometimes fifteen minutes was all I had.

The first week I visited the gorgeous gardens, I enjoyed the heated tropical greenhouse. The next week, I attended the orchid exhibition. The week after that, the bluebells were out and were glorious; the following week the tulips, roses and so on. Each week I was noticing – noticing nature, colour, texture, natural art exhibitions, changes in weather, my surroundings. I became aware that there was so much change in nature.

Over the months, as I kept visiting and enjoying the space, I began to relax. My body began to unwind. I had previously suffered from stress-related sciatica. With exercise, walking in Kew and relaxation, it gradually lessened. I became aware that I was enjoying observing nature and being aware of my surroundings. At work, my workshop design began to improve, my energy was improving, and my facilitation seemed better and easier.

Noticing nature in my surroundings has become more of a habit now – I'm not great at it, but I am better at pausing and smelling plants, seeing colours, noticing change. It slows me down and relaxes me – it really shifts my mood. I am still committed to going to Kew each week. It was the best financial and time investment I've made this year.

TECHNIQUES

Noticing nature

Begin to notice nature around you at work and on your daily commute. If there is little to notice, could you adapt your travel route to go somewhere more appealing? Could you arrange to spend time in a park, in the woods, by the sea or similar during your week?

When you are in nature, pay attention to colours, light, surroundings and temperature. Be present.

G: GIVE – 'Your time. Your words. Your presence.'[24]

We know from research that helping others can help you feel good[25], encourage endorphins, bring a sense of belonging and reduce isolation. In my experience, helping others when you don't expect anything in return:

- Gives you a sense of empathy that makes life feel truly easier
- Helps to keep things in perspective, by moving the focus away from your own challenges and stressful thoughts
- Helps make the world a happier place – and it's contagious

Global Generosity Challenge

In 2016, inspired by my colleague and friend, Wayne, a group of us decided to take part in a generosity challenge created by Nipun Metha.[26] I decided to take part with a local group of a dozen colleagues. The aim was to carry out one different, generous action each day for twenty-one days. We had a weekly support group led by one of our team. We discussed our experiences: the different ways we were practising being generous, what we were thinking and how we were feeling about our resistance or enthusiasm.

During my twenty-one days I opened doors, bought free drinks and lunch, gave up seats on buses. I noticed that after Day 14, we all struggled to find *new ways to be generous* – it was a real stretch to be creative. That's because the group and I were generous in the *ways we were used to*. We began to create a list of new possible generous actions to inspire us to keep going.

Through neuroscience we have now learnt that the brain has plasticity; that we can build new neural pathways by learning and changing habits. And here we all were on our Global Generosity Challenge, in the process of creating new habits – maybe even building new neural pathways. We made it to Day 21. We all found the challenge tough, beneficial and heart-warming. But I noticed that giving was both natural and a stretch. I'm so glad I took part in the challenge – I don't think I changed long-term habits, but it reminded me that as humans, we are naturally generous and that we needed to be more innovative. The Global Generosity Challenge is an inexpensive way to be less focused on your own challenges in life and at work. Therefore it lends itself to helping you be more resilient.

Evidence shows that the benefits of helping others can last long after the act itself and are one of the strongest routes to well-being. Believe it or not, studies show this can even help us live longer. But in my experience, it has to be giving *from the heart*, not in some duty-bound way.

TECHNIQUES

Reflecting on giving at work

a. Sit back and reflect: What small action could you take to build on your generosity with a colleague? Could you give time at work, offer support to a colleague, be kinder and more generous with a client or customer?

b. When someone next talks to you at work, give your presence, turn away from your computer or other distraction and give them your full attention.

Luxury and survival

Research shows that applying the Five Ways of Well-Being makes a significant contribution to your fulfilment life, even when all other demographics are taken into account. When you feel fulfilled, you might find you can be more flexible and that you have the inner strength to persist at work with adversity, people you previously found challenging and new, challenging goals. You might experience that obstacles 'go over your head' in a new way.

At the heart of well-being and resilience at work are the environment (the support and good practices an employer puts in place) and your individual commitment to take better care of yourself. Your commitment can be a series of small steps – from moments of doing nothing but noticing, to being generous in action.

The Dalai Lama tells us, 'Just as ripples spread out when a single pebble is dropped into water, the actions of individuals can have far-reaching effects.'[27] Even small well-being actions at work can have a ripple effect on your inner strength, your staying power and perhaps on your colleagues' resilience as well. Keep in mind that nurturing your well-being – on the journey to resilience – is not a luxury: it is both urgent and important.

Tips: Five Ways of Well-Being at Work

I think the Five Ways of Well-Being speak for themselves, whether in the workplace or in your wider life:

- Connect
- Keep learning
- Be active
- Keep noticing
- Keep giving

3: Changing Mindsets

- **'I don't know what to do next.'**
- **'I'm not sure I can keep going.'**
- **'I am nervous of change.'**
- **'I'm not willing to compromise.'**
- **'I'm definitely not going to change my plan.'**
- **'I'm all over the place with all the changes coming up.'**
- **'It's all so difficult, this uncertainty and change.'**
- **'Everyone's saying it's going to get worse – I agree.'**
- **'We talk about the problem a lot, but there are no solutions emerging.'**

If you are feeling unsettled about future change and uncertainty, it helps to do some mindset work. Mindsets, 'a person's way of thinking and their opinions'[28] the accumulation of thoughts, along with the emotion behind them that forms opinions and eventually, beliefs. If you've been spending time thinking about 'what's going wrong' and feel stuck in a rut, focusing on this inner resilience can be useful. Alternatively, if you are faced with a persistent or repetitive challenge that you can't quite shake off, inner mindset work can be beneficial. Working on your thinking can bring a profound sense of calm and well-being to your working and wider life.

You might have gathered so far that there are various skills that help your resilience at work:

- Awareness of how resilient you are feeling
- Choosing your resilience aim
- Taking care of your well-being

Here we will address how awareness of your thinking and working to explore it can help you be both more flexible and determined. This mindset learning is part of being REALLY RESILIENT, as it grounds you, gets you mentally 'unstuck' and gets you ready for action. We will look at various mindset approaches, beginning with the cycle of change.

The Change Game

New experiences, challenges, initiating disruptive change and general change are part of working life for many people. For some people, it's what they live for – it's like a game they are learning to play. In my experience, even people who live for change, often need to foster self-care around resilience: checking in on energy levels and well-being so they avoid burnout. For others, change, unexpected change and the move towards a more disruptive and innovative workplace culture, are experienced as more of a challenge.

When you are feeling less resilient, or less versed in resilient thinking and actions, these types of changes are harder to bear. It can be hard to feel positive and harder to bounce forward from new unforeseen difficulties. Everyone has times when they might perceive change as challenging, as a demand for innovation, as unforeseen failures, impossible obstacles, rather than things to overcome. We may feel quite mixed; I often find I have an immediate, welcoming excitement about change, followed by a deeper, thoughtful worry mindset. At last, I seem to settle on recognising that it's good, or that I can handle whatever is new.

Many changes are outside of our control, although we may often be able to influence the direction we aim for and also influence other people. In my experience, aiming to change or control others brings a lifetime of stress and disappointment. Often when we focus on 'what we want', we need to check in and see that what we are aiming for is not a question of control, e.g. 'I want X to change'. It's better and more realistic to have something focused on us, e.g. 'I want to learn to work better with X.' Definitely within our control to influence – with time and effort – is our *mindset*. Resilience enables us to better cope with change by finding ways to have a more flexible, adaptable mindset. It also gives us the skill of tapping into determination as a mindset, so that we can persist in the face of change or obstacles.

From pushing away to embracing

Many people have a reaction to change where they would like to avoid it or push it away and keep things working as they were. Over time and with work your mindset and feelings can shift from the more difficult mindsets to being more embracing, positive and accepting. Working with the cycle of change is one approach that embodies this shift.

The cycle of change is well known in the world of learning and change management. It is underpinned by decades of work by Elizabeth Kübler-Ross.[29] It helps you see how you react and respond to new and different and unexpected experiences. It highlights how we can move through stages of changing mindsets and emotional states – from feeling shocked or surprised to acceptance and new inspired choices. We may not all go through the same stages, but we tend to have a psychological reaction to adversity and it's the learning from this that can help us be more resilient.

The cycle of change image below for example, is my depiction of the emotional and psychological stages I went through when I lost both my jobs within a few weeks of each other.

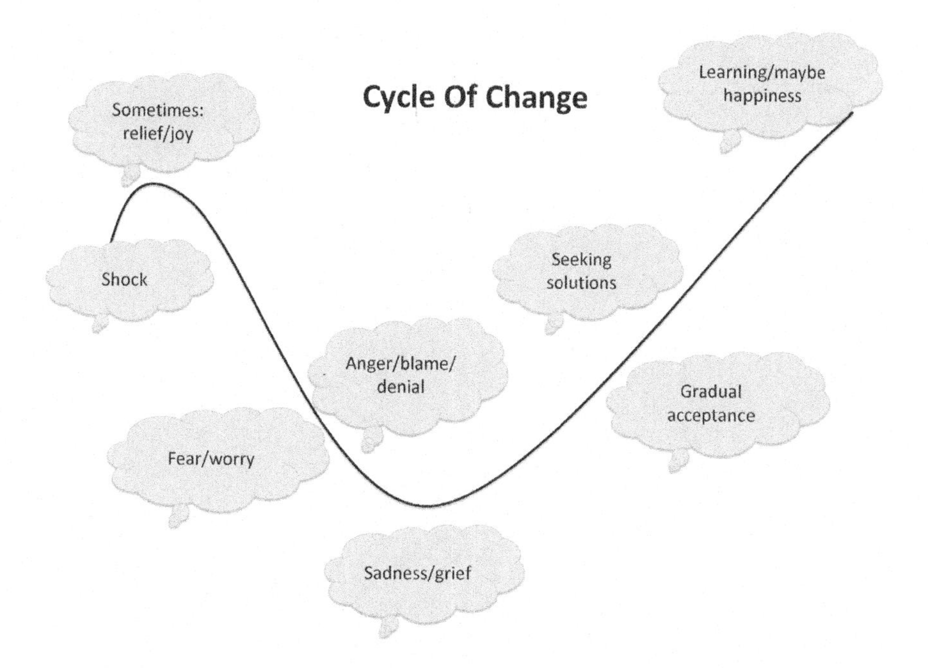

I went on a journey using many different techniques to support me to survive and eventually thrive. Most people can identify at least one big change they went through at work that was hard to adjust to. They can, with reflection, recall what they did to support themselves through change. So this second image contains the techniques I used that enabled me to accept and adjust to the change – to be more resilient. To bounce forward to a new career stage. It's good to do this, as you end up with a list of strategies that have helped you to be more resilient to adversity in the past. That is something you can draw on.

Here is what helped me to move through the challenging journey:

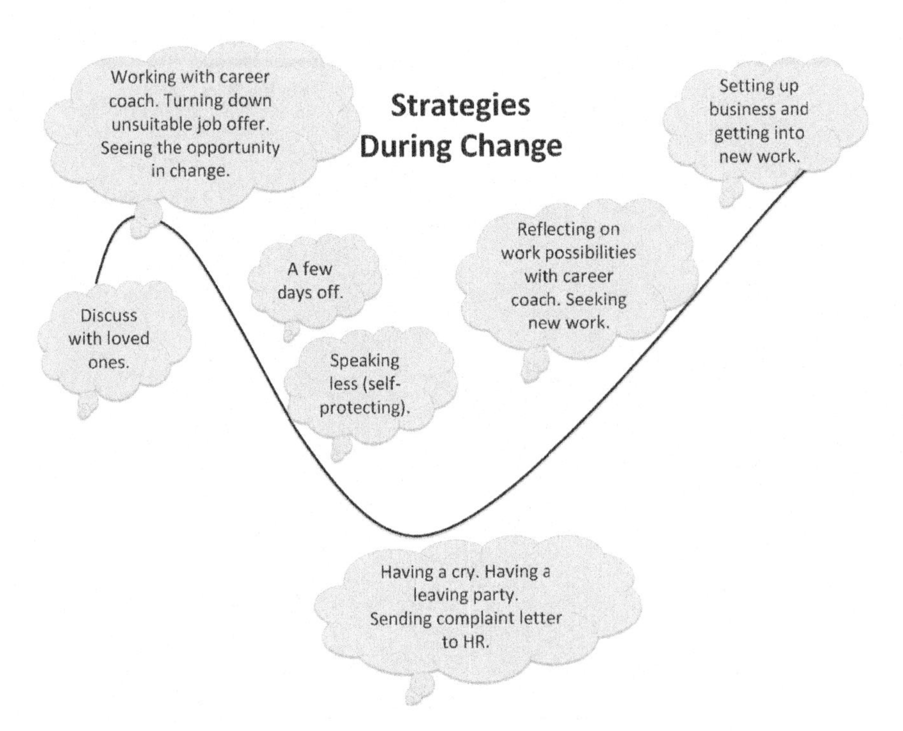

For me one of the keys things was that, despite the huge loss of the jobs I enjoyed and colleagues I loved, there was *opportunity* in the changes. I could finally be freelance and as much as I liked my line manager, I'd now get to be my own boss.

When I teach the change cycle in workshops, it is important to highlight that there is also a *positive change cycle* – where you are simply excited from the beginning and there are few or no negative moments. Obviously, change that isn't instigated by you is harder to handle as it may feel out of your control.

Here's an example of the more positive change cycle. I often experience this when working on a big project.

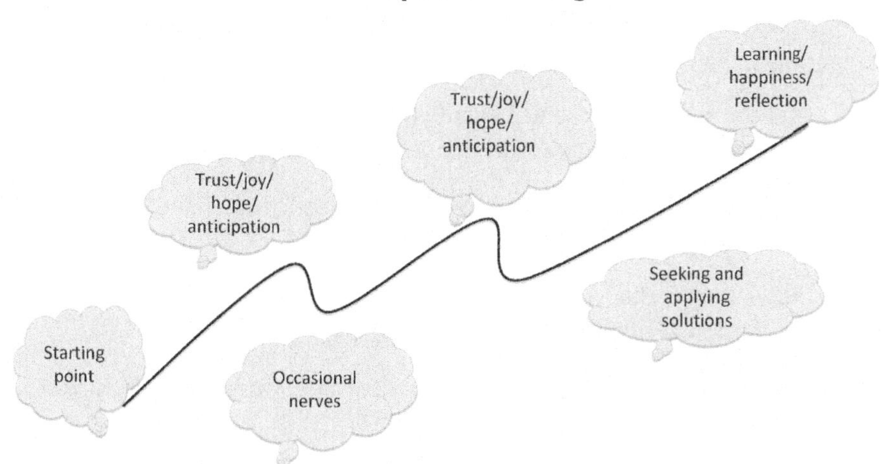

TECHNIQUES

Reflecting on your cycle of change

- Reflect on a past challenge or change at work that you found difficult but learned to adjust to or accept.
- Take a piece of paper and draw your own change cycle model, including the stages you went through.
- Reflect on what or who helped you to move through the process of change or challenge. Add that into your diagram.
- Sit back and ponder this experience for a few minutes – the journey, the learning and the success.
- How might the strategies you used help you with any current disruption, challenge or change?
- Using your reflection, identify a small step for change, to help you handle your current challenge.

As you work on your cycle of change examples, practise accepting the idea that new experiences, challenges and change are part of working life. Certain goals may no longer be possible. Certain tasks or roles may no longer be needed and that may impact on you. Notice that you have often survived change. Working on accepting the 'new' and circumstances that *cannot* be changed, can help you focus on circumstances that you *can* influence and alter.

Keeping your eye on the horizon

Tied in with this is the value of keeping your eye on the horizon, on emerging trends and new changes. This is not the same as assuming you know the future; it is more like sensing and noticing emerging change. This is a key skill highlighted by Professor Otto Scharmer and Katrin Kaufer from MIT, where you learn to listen deeply to yourself and others and to ask questions about what trends and changes are emerging on the horizon, so you can sense how to innovate.[30]

For example, at the moment, in terms of changing working environments, I see that co-working spaces are growing and that at best they are strong communities and at the least they are practical places to work. They help many previously isolated people to feel connected and part of a community. Right now the horizon is:

- the global growth of co-working spaces
- the emergence of a booming flexi-work-from-home culture
- the growing number of freelancers
- an increasing sense of isolation (in terms of mental well-being) and so an increasing need to connect at work

It pays keep your eye on the horizon – not in a stressful way, but just to be aware of current changes and trends. It means you may feel less taken aback by some changes. In Chapter 4: Launch and Take Action, you'll learn techniques to help you relax and questions to ask yourself about what is on the horizon.

Solutions-Focused Conversations

- 'My work conversations are always going round in circles.'
- 'Our team meetings don't resolve anything.'
- 'I hear myself complaining all the time.'
- 'I can't seem to fix the problem.'

Does any of this sound familiar? Have you ever noticed that many workplace conversations focus on what isn't working well rather than what is? In my workshop and coaching experience, it's usual for people who feel stuck at work to ruminate on the problems themselves, spending more time thinking about those and less on finding potential solutions. Perhaps it's actually easier to go round in circles, exploring who is to blame, how hard it is and how you feel about it. I've done that for much of my life and often do it when stressed. Talking over difficulties has its place, but with resilience building, we need a *change of mindset* to help us move forward.

Your mindset is a powerful frame and lens for your perception of challenges. Thinking and having conversations generate solutions, releasing you from the blame game and helping you identify what could be done now to adapt or adjust. Working with Solutions-Focused philosophy, thinking and conversations means discovering that there are *possibilities for change* in nearly every experience. I've used Solutions-Focused thinking thousands of times over the last twelve years. Solutions-Focused as an approach is popular in many public and private sectors, as a way to shift mindsets and help teams become more effective. Solutions-Focused is a deeply evidence-based approach, developed by Insoo Kim Berg and Steve de Shazer.[31]

Here is a simple example to illustrate the difference between the common types of questions that we might habitually ask others – or ourselves – when we're facing a challenge or obstacle and a Solutions-Focused question:

- Typical Problem-Focused question: 'What's the problem?' and, 'What's wrong?'
- Typical Solutions-Focused question: 'What are you aiming for?' and, 'What do you want?'

Solutions-Focused simply focuses on possibilities for change. It's more directed towards what has worked in the past, is working now and could work in the future as a way to resolve challenges.

A way to experiment with Solutions-Focused is to practise the Solutions Thinking activity below. Over time, you may be able to see how this enables you to find a way forward, feel and be more resourceful, identify small steps for change and take action – all good resilience skills.

TECHNIQUES

Solutions Thinking

Set up: You can do this almost anywhere as long as you have a few moments of quiet.

Activity: Bring to mind a particular challenge, difficulty or problem. Spend a few minutes considering what bothers you about it, who is to blame, how it is a challenge and how you feel. Next, with the same challenge in mind:

- Think about what you are aiming for. Choose something within your area of control, not regarding others' feelings or behaviours, e.g. 'I want X to do better at Y.' Instead, select something more self-focused, e.g. 'I want to learn to better influence X to do better at Y.' Instead of, 'I want X to stop turning up late to our meetings' you could have 'I want to learn to better teach X about time management'. Then the change is focused on *you*. In Solutions-Focused thinking, this is called you being a 'customer for change' – someone who wants change and is prepared to do something about it .
- Envisage what life will look like when the solution is in place.
- Recall similar challenges you have resolved in the past and what you did to resolve them.
- Reflect on all the qualities you have to solve challenges.
- Now identify a small step to take to work towards your current goal.
- Finally, reflect on or write down the challenges, issues and goals you face in your organisation. Where might Solutions-Focused questions help you shift your thinking? How could you bring a Solutions-Focused approach into any team meetings? What value would that bring?

Changing perspective using humour

I've always appreciated good comedians. From Billy Connolly, Sarah Millican and Richard Pryor to Nina Conti, I love to laugh. I've learned that many comedians have challenging or complex pasts, yet they bring humour to it.

Tapping into humour – your own or appreciating that of others – is a powerful mindset tool. I've noticed how much humour has helped my mental resilience. It gives me a new, easier perspective and lightens my thinking. Have you ever noticed that in your own thinking? My team and I often laugh at ourselves – the challenges, the obstacles, the setbacks. When our perspective becomes blocked, humour seems to broaden our view, lighten the load and give space for emotions to flow. The significant positive effect of humour in resiliency at work and lessening the chances of burnout has been cited in a nursing study.[32]

I've always considered myself as a serious person, especially at work. But over the last two years, I've noticed my clients and I are laughing more in coaching conversations. It's like I decided to bring the humour in and gradually it seeps into our conversations at exactly the right time. Furthermore, this year during my first big keynote speech, I discovered I could be funny. The audience were laughing – not at me but with me. It was a turning point. Not only did I appreciate humour but I was being humorous.

Discovering your inner comedian is sadly beyond the boundaries of this book. But if tapping into humour to change your perspective is of interest to you, you could begin with some simple steps:

- Spend an hour watching your favourite stand-up comedian to shift your mind and mood from a challenging subject.
- Spend time with people who you really laugh with and talk about the challenging topics with the intention of bringing some humour in. Does it lighten the mood?
- Intentionally be more humorous at work – practise smiling authentically, perhaps during a presentation or conversation. Try out little safe, appropriate jokes until you feel more confident.

Reality thinking – drama versus reality

Let's try another kind of thinking that really gets you moving. 'Reality thinking' is a way of aligning yourself, so that reality (what's actually happening) and your thoughts match up. (There are some overlaps here with Cognitive Behavioural Therapy[33] and 'objective thinking'). In my experience, this alignment creates less mental stress. There are times in life when you are mentally stuck in dramatic, painful, magnifying or judgemental thoughts that for simplicity I will refer to as dramatic 'narratives'. Dramatic thinking is more compelling than reality. I recall reading once that learning to think in narratives is a skill we learn as a child. Below are various types of painful narratives – making a skewed story from reality:

- Dramatizing: 'It's all awful.'
- Predicting: 'It's going to get worse.'
- Judging and blaming: 'It's their fault.'
- Controlling: 'They should think/feel/do X.'

Sometimes these thoughts may be true, but often they may differ from reality in subtle or obvious ways. When it comes to resilience, the problem with this dramatic skewed thinking is that it generates stress and uses up energy (including your persistence energy, your staying power) and can deeply influence the actions you take. This is known as thought-emotion-behaviour cycle. Additionally, skewed thinking may not help you find solutions, because you are stressed and running on adrenaline. Finally, it's *rigid* thinking, so it lacks flexibility – the key quality of resilience.

Evidence shows that some challenges are useful for building resilience. Challenges help us to grow and put us under pressure, which is useful for our development. However, ongoing long-term challenge can be both stressful and damaging over time – using up energy, leaving you feeling worn out and defensive. I know that if I want to be more resilient at work, it helps to have more *accurate evidence-based thinking* and therefore less stress. I can't control the outside stuff, but I can work on my thinking. That way, I can have freer thinking. Often it's our perception of events, not the event itself, that is the cause of many of our stresses. For example, if my perception of unexpected change is it's challenging, stressful and problematic, while others in a similar situation experience the same change as an 'opportunity', it must be *my* thinking and therefore *my* perception that is making the difference. So as a starting point, awareness of your thinking is key.

Being with reality – negotiating

Here's an example: I had recently been negotiating a learning programme. I was feeling stressed about the way we were moving forward and I believed my client was amending the informal rules of our agreement. I felt they were being unethical – it was a conflict and I wanted to either give up or control them.

Here is a list of my thoughts:

- They are unethical.
- They keep being pushy.
- If only they would do X...
- I dislike them.
- It's too messy.
- I don't want to work with them.

Noticing my thoughts and having a conversation about my thinking created a small gap between my thoughts and myself. This is the power of observation. It somehow felt a little less stressful, as I felt less controlled by my thoughts and more an observer of them.

TECHNIQUES

Noticing stressful thoughts (the foundation for Reality Thinking)

Set up: It's best to do this *outside* of work, as it can bring up strong feelings that you might need a bit of space to process.

Activity: Bring to mind one stressful topic. Write down your thoughts about it, including all the 'shoulds', future predictions, and judgements about the other person, e.g. 'X should do Y' and 'This is too hard. I can't cope. It will become even harder.'

Look at the list. See it as separate from you. It's your *thinking* rather than *you*. Together – as a group of thoughts – it is your perception. Notice that. That perception shapes your emotions. That shapes your behaviour. Pause and breathe. Notice that cycle: thinking-emotions-behaviour.

TECHNIQUES

Reality Thinking (and Possibility Thinking)[34]

If you are keen to go a step further, try Reality Thinking – sometimes called Possibility Thinking. It's based on being curious about your thoughts. This is a way to help release the power of stressful thoughts over you.[35]

Set up: Again this technique is ideally done away from your usual work environment. Perhaps in a café over a cup of tea.

Activity: Take one of your stressful thoughts – from the activity above – and gently and kindly put it under a metaphorical 'magnifying glass', asking, 'Is it true? Is it possible that it might not be as true as I thought?' You could rephrase the stressful sentence with a prefix or suffix: 'He should' could become conditional, e.g. 'Maybe he should…' With 'I can't cope' you could add a question onto the end, e.g. 'I can't cope, can I?' You could put a thought into the past: 'I used to think…' You could add uncertainty to a thought 'It may be true that…' Finally, you could add possibility: 'Maybe…' That way your stressful thoughts are 'less certain' and perhaps less judgemental.

Review: See how these new thoughts sit with you. Do they feel less stressful? Ask yourself if it's possible that they could be true. Could they be as real *or true* as your previous stressful thoughts? Or are they even truer? Do they represent reality better, rather than the previous internal drama?

These new thoughts embrace different possibilities. I am not a huge fan of positive thinking, but 'possibility thinking'[36] is a good resilience building skill. In time with practise, you may notice your old habitual stressful thoughts arising and you may question them kindly and regularly with curiosity. If you do this authentically, you may notice some of your habitual ways of thinking are loosened – you might feel more relaxed and less stressed.

Changing the Lens – Learning the Lesson and Seeing the Opportunity[37]

Finally, I'd like to help you see an experience of how to change your mindset to embracing a challenge rather than resisting – again without doing 'positive thinking'.

This technique is summed up as, 'Changing the Lens, Learning the Lesson and Seeing the Opportunity' – the lens being your frame of perception. Perceiving the deeper lesson or opportunity in any experience helps your resilience, as it frees your thinking and enables you to have a clearer sense of direction. So you have more energy and less mental stress. Instead of the key skill being curiosity here, the skill here is *stepping back and seeing what the lesson is* in any situation. Here's an example:

Connecting back to my example about negotiating a learning programme process I was going through (TECHNIQUES: Noticing stressful thoughts), in a reflective journey on a train, I realised that the negotiation process represented that chance to stand up for myself and be a clear and straightforward communicator. That was the deeper lesson. My thoughts, although they were useful, were different under this new lens. Don't get me wrong – I didn't change my thinking. I noticed I was perceiving the situation differently, once I saw that it represented an opportunity to improve my negotiation skills and to be clear. Once I anonymised it and looked at it from a lesson and opportunity level rather than a personal level, here's how I began to perceive things:

Previous thought	New way of thinking
They are unethical.	*They have different ethics to me. I will not compromise on mine.*
They keep being pushy.	*They are a better negotiator than I am. I'll learn to be better. I might find later as my skills improve,that I can create a workshop on 'Ethical negotiation'.*
If only they would do X...	*I'm getting to learn about standing up for myself and be a clearer communicator.*
I dislike them.	*I see that they are different and I am curious about that.*
It's too messy.	*I am choosing to be clear in business, because it matters to me.*
I don't want to work with them.	*If I continue to be clear, I am willing to work with them. If I don't get anything agreed, I am happy to walk away and at least I have learnt some new lessons and skills.*

As my thinking changed, my sense of direction became clearer. In reality I was choosing a new client group and a deeper level of negotiation. Suddenly, it didn't seem so much of a hassle to learn this valuable life lesson. My stress level dropped and I felt I could now keep negotiating with ease. I felt my ability to see this process through had returned.

TECHNIQUES

Changing the Lens, Learning the Lesson

Set up: this is a nice reflection to do when sitting away from your desk. A relaxed space or co-working lounge area would be ideal.

Activity: Bring to mind any stressful workplace experience – not the most stressful or raw experience though, as that will be too tough for this technique and it may feel unkind. Now, imagine you could step back and watch the experience, as if you have a bird's eye view of it. Watch it as if you were watching a movie of the experience. Rather than focus on individuals, ask yourself: 'What am I learning through this experience/challenge?' and 'What do I need to learn from this experience/challenge?'

What occurs to you when you ask these questions?

Now, see if you are willing to look at the experience/challenge as something that you can learn from (I'm not saying you attracted it in any way or that you have to be a martyr. Or even that you have to put up with awful behaviour by others at work by looking only at the lesson). Ask yourself if there is space within you for the lesson to be absorbed, even if it's a harsh lesson to learn. You might find that you are too irritated or angry for this. But sit with this way of exploring the experience for a while and see what happens.

Closing check out: Explore what happens when you think in this way. Does it free you up even a little? Does it inspire any new feelings or perceptions?

Changing Mindsets summary

So there you have it: four different ways to work with your perception and mindset. It's so enjoyable to do this work with your thoughts. In time you will notice that you have these new techniques that you can apply to *any* work challenge. On workshops, I also teach how you can apply these enhanced ways of thinking to teams. We explore how leaders and managers can support their team's resilience. There is always more opportunity for learning; if encouragement and good resilience modelling comes from managers, it can only enhance the workplace.

For now, if you have a manager or team and they are not ready for a new mindset, practise your own awareness raising (noticing your thoughts) and then adapt thoughts using 'Solutions Thinking', 'Reality Thinking' or 'Learning the Lesson'. Learn the skills yourself – it will only make you stronger.

Tips: Changing Mindsets

- Consider a change you have been through. Draw your own change cycle. Be curious about what enabled you to move forward.
- Pause and notice your thoughts more often.
- Tap into humour and change your perspective, by watching some comedy.
- Work with the Solutions-Focused questions for a new outlook.
- Use curiosity thinking – in a gentle but persistent way, ask yourself, 'Is this really, absolutely true?'
- Apply 'learning the lesson' thinking to any current (not too raw) stressful experience.

4: Launch and Take Action

- **'I feel stuck.'**
- **'There are so many obstacles.'**
- **'I'm not getting anywhere.'**
- **'I'm running out of steam.'**
- **'I feel inflexible.'**
- **'I can't decide what to do.'**
- **'How do I get moving with this problem?'**
- **'I can't say no to more responsibility, more challenges, more stress.'**
- **'I've had enough. Maybe it's time to leave?'**

Do any of these 'stuck places' sound like your situation or your thinking? If so, this chapter is for you.

To help you become more resilient we will focus on how to get unstuck using Solutions-Focused small steps and by tapping into being more relaxed before you make decisions. Sometimes action can be enabled by you being more flexible – a true resilience skill. So we will focus on how you can find your way to a more flexible approach. We will then explore staying power – digging deep and being determined and persistent. Finally, we will explore those times when you feel you might have had enough – and what to do in those moments.

Getting unstuck

Every time I teach coaching skills workshops, we talk about the fact that coaching balances both action and reflection. During the coaching session, you are given space to reflect on the topic that's particularly challenging. Hopefully you find a way forward. Towards the end of the session, we work towards identifying actions that you could potentially take. You will carry these out between conversations. So the model is 'reflection and action'. Otherwise, if you are not doing actions, you're just having a cosy reflective chat. That's not coaching and that's certainly not being resilient.

Quite often in coaching, my coachees know what the solutions are, but they are unclear about what the first small step should be. Have you ever been in this situation? Being resilient often means not just knowing what to do but *taking steps* for change. Otherwise your mind might be resilient, but nothing much changes in the outside world.

Solutions-Focused philosophy (see Chapter 3) teaches us that often there are big goals we mentally commit to that we sometimes do nothing about. But it's the actions that count, as they build resilience. It often feels easier to carry out a small step than to take one big action; you can get unstuck and moving with small steps. It may be less like the dramatic actions of movies, but small steps are often what real life is made of. My Post-Graduate Certificate of Education, for example, was the result of hundreds and thousands of small steps taken over a year. Even when we didn't have a lecture, my peer study group met each week, reading a chapter of a book for discussion. We were the only group that did this. This small step we took each week resulted in us all being more widely informed for our assignments and our research. Ultimately it helped me achieve my bigger goal: my teaching qualification.

TECHNIQUES

Small steps for change

When you know the direction you want to take, but feel a bit overwhelmed, there are a couple of Solutions-Focused questions that might be useful to help you take small steps.

Set up: You can carry this out simply by thinking it through, but it's best done with pen and paper. You need five to ten minutes, ideally at work, so you are in the environment you are focusing on.

Activity: Take a moment and bring to mind the challenge or goal. Scribble a few notes about it to give you a bit of context:

- What you want
- What your strategy is to get there
- Remind yourself of all your skills you have that you will use to help you on the journey towards this goal

Now ask yourself – what's the *smallest step* I could take towards this, in the next few days? Choose from:

- Small steps you *have taken before*, that have worked in the past
- The *easiest* small step
- The *most likely to succeed*
- A *random* choice
- What seems *intuitively* right

Making sure it is practical and measurable, write down your one small step you commit to taking in the next few days. Add your small step to your diary, so that you can check in with yourself on the day it's to be done – it's a way of reminding yourself to take action. Alternatively, you can let a colleague know what your small step is. Tell them you will check in with them when it's done. It's a way of staying accountable.

I'll close this section with a great quote from Gary Jones, ex-Deputy Principal of Highland's College in Jersey: 'Solutions-Focused coaching is about small actions that happen immediately, rather than big objectives that never happen.'[38]

Getting moving by tapping into the best decisions

If you tap into your real inner insight (your intuition) before you take decisions about actions, then your actions are more likely to make a positive impact at work. Connected with this is the need to keep your eye on any changes emerging on the horizon. If you practise this combination, your intuition is more likely to tell you what to do next for a grounded, clear, relaxed space. MIT professor Otto Scharmer calls this 'tapping into the source' – the place where your 'inner wisdom' taps into what feels right in the face of challenge, change and emerging trends[39]. Otto Scharmer and Katrin Kaufer also note in their groundbreaking book, *Leading from the Emerging Future,* that these insights and actions have a higher likelihood of a greater positive impact. They are different from habitual insights, solutions and reactions that usually leave us recreating the same old solutions to challenges, and get us the same old unsuccessful results. [40]

At work, when you are relaxed, feeling inspired or working in a team with healthy levels of communication and collaboration, it's much easier to tap into your gut feeling or intuition and be clear about what actions to take. Relaxation seems to give a direct link to your intuition and also creates space for you to feel more flexible and adaptable. However, sometimes we need to use certain techniques to achieve relaxation. So, rather than rushing to a stressful meeting, or rushing to make a decision about something, take five minutes out and perform the following easy visualisation/ relaxation exercise.

Relaxing using Qigong

Qigong is an ancient type of soft martial art, similar to Tai Chi but with less set moves. It's used all over the world for both healing and well-being. I studied Hua Gong, a form of Qigong whilst working as a volunteer in the Gateway Clinic, Southwestern Hospital, a Chinese Medicine Clinic on the NHS. The Gateway Clinic did groundbreaking work in well-being and natural medicine around substance abuse, HIV and challenging healthcare issues. Whilst there, I qualified in auricular acupuncture and reflexology, and studied Chinese Food Therapy, Body Acupuncture and Qigong. Each working day began with one hour of Qigong and ended with a ninety-minute session. It was immersive learning. The following Inner Smile meditation is so easy to do and is both uplifting and relaxing. It gives you a sense of 'spaciousness' that's useful before decision making. Experiment with the meditation before deciding on any action.

TECHNIQUES

Inner smile – from Qigong practice

The Inner Smile practice is a wonderful way to brighten up your day and relax you so you can hear your intuition (you might call this gut feeling or inner knowledge). It's also great to help you tap into clarity about how to be adaptable.

Set up: Use this practice at lunch break – you can put on some headphones and sit on a comfortable chair. You need between five and twenty-five minutes.

Activity: Settle into your chair and notice your in-breath and out-breath. Don't change your breathing, just notice it. Then smile gently and imagine the smile going all the way to your belly, brightening up your whole body.

See if you can accept however the mediation goes – it may feel easy, hard, or slow. Rather than forcing a smile, give permission for a little more relaxation. You might notice as you smile, that your breathing relaxes and slows down. But don't change the breathing on purpose. Let the smile fill your whole body. If you get distracted, bring yourself gently back and carry on.

This relaxation can be a great way to start and finish the working day, or before a stressful meeting. It can also be done whilst walking. If you're in a hurry, make it a minute or two in length. It's also a way to tap into a calm decision-making mood hence, used with the following questions, it can generate your ideas around adaptability and flexibility.

Deciding on the inspired action: When you have finished your meditation, bring to mind a current situation, issue or challenge and ask yourself these questions:

- What does my inner knowledge (intuition, gut feeling or insight) tell me about the right course of action regarding this issue?
- What does my inner knowledge (intuition, gut feeling or insight) tell me is the first small step to take?
- What does my inner knowledge (intuition, gut feeling or insight) tell me about being adaptable and flexible (in this situation)?

Getting flexible with compromise

We all reach a point where what we want doesn't seem achievable at work. There are the usual restrictions, like not having enough resources; or people we find difficult; or rules and regulations that make life hard; or even opportunities that don't come to fruition. Sometimes, in the name of moving forward and being resilient to these obstacles, we need to learn to be flexible through compromise.

Flexibility includes the skill of compromise. Not a begrudging compromise, but an openhearted, openminded willingness to negotiate; to flex our goal or direction. It might include giving up some of what you want in the hope that other person gives up some of what they want too. That way you both end up with something that includes some, but not all, of your needs. I'm not particularly great at compromise but I've learnt that it's a way to be resilient. I still get most of what I want. Compromising really means 'splitting the difference'.

A flexibility story: Funding and compromise

A simple example of learning flexibility at work was when I needed to source some external coaching for thirty organisational managers. We could apply for funding, but the compromise was that the fund was for focusing on discussing leadership of a particular UK diploma that might be taking place in the next few years. I took the fund information to a senior manager and she showed me how beautifully she could flex and adapt the application response and the purpose. We focused on the value of a broad range of skills needed to set up the diploma. So she argued the conversations could include leadership conversations *in general,* as well as those related to the diploma. She was right. It was a broader picture. What I compromised on was my perfectionism, and on insisting that all the managers focused on the diploma at all times. But I didn't compromise my value of authenticity. Our application was successful.

What I gained was the opportunity for thirty managers to receive coaching on leadership skills and for some or all of the managers to include diploma discussions as part of those conversations. With my perfectionist standards, it wasn't ideal, but it was a healthy compromise and it achieved the purpose of resourcing managers.

In the end, the diplomas were dropped as an educational qualification in the UK, so it was good that we had expanded the view to focus on general leadership skills instead. I learnt from that senior manager how to compromise in practice, without compromising values.

TECHNIQUES

Getting flexible with compromise

Set up: Find a moment to reflect – either sitting or walking. You'll need about five to ten minutes at a time when you won't be interrupted.

Activity: Think of a situation where you are working on a project or activity with someone and it appears that your visions of what success looks like are different. Ask yourself these questions (and if you like, write down your answers):

- What do I want or need?
- What does/might the other person want or need?
- What solutions are already emerging?
- What is the thing I could let go of from my needs?
- What need or want am I not willing to let go of?
- What might this situation look like from the other person's perspective?
- What solutions seem possible? How do I feel about those and why?
- Am I willing to compromise?
- Would I be happy with X or Y type of compromise?
- What now seems the best way forward?
- How can I best communicate this, the next time we speak or meet?

By reflecting on your feelings and needs around compromise, you can learn to move forward without a begrudging attitude. In this way you become more resilient, as you learn to be truly flexible.

Digging Deep and Getting Persistent

Sometimes the energy required to complete something is greater than you first thought and you need to dig deep to get it done. That's a good reason to persist.

There are extreme times when you just don't have energy to keep going. You're exhausted. Your resilience is at rock bottom. These are the times to rest and recoup your energy, or to learn to say no – a boundary skill. Sometimes it is even time to learn to leave – leave the job, project or employer – more about that below. In the moments when you need to rest and recoup, read Chapter 2 and put the well-being actions and mindsets into practice.

At other times, it may not be possible to stop. You may need to keep going, perhaps for the short term or medium term to achieve your goal. Then you can recover your energy afterwards. This isn't an advisable strategy for the long term, as it may lead to burn out. But we all do it sometimes.

There are occasions when I have persisted with a particular direction, despite the emotional or physical fallout on relationships or myself. This may have caused upset about my choices and direction, but the stakes were too high, my values too compromised if I stopped. So I kept going. During these times, it pays to keep asking yourself if the potential fallout is worth persisting: 'Is the possible gain still worth more than the possible loss?' 'Do I want to, or need to still keep going?'

Here are some ideas for the times when you need to keep going despite obstacles.

Lightness and humour

My experience is that sometimes if you can persist in a more light-hearted way by bringing humour to the table, you may feel more resilient. For example, when I was writing this book I took the advice of two colleagues. Anny and Kyle[41] both told me to stop aiming to write an excellent book and just write. Kyle said 'Write average stuff – it's okay to do that.' Anny said 'Aim to write the worst book you can.' Their comments made me smile, and bought ease to writing. I couldn't quite go as far as aiming to write the worst book, but I knew if I aimed to write an average book, I would get going. That mindset helped me to shift my previous struggle (I'd made three unsuccessful attempts) and the writing flowed. I went from struggling to writing a few pages, to finding it easy to write a chapter and then a whole book.

Persistence – memory and questions

If you want to be persistent at work, you also need to create more and more experiences where you learn to stand up for yourself and stick to your guns, keep going and don't give up. Not in a sociopathic way, (e.g. 'I don't care who this harms') but with clarity about what you want, what they want and practice in reasserting your needs and direction. That way you accumulate experiences of persistence, which form part of your memory bank. Determination then becomes easier to tap into as it's in your subconscious and conscious memory bank.

Solutions-Focused philosophy (see Chapter 3) asks you to tap into previous success in life, in order to keep going. This seems odd but it really works. It's a nice memory tool.

One of my colleagues, Eric Decker, told me about a piece of research that proved that if you feel more resourceful before you commit to action, you are more likely to carry out the action, to follow through. I found this one of the most powerful precursors to taking action at work, especially where I had previously doubted myself. This approach seems like common sense, but actually it's something that we often miss out.

For example, at work if I'm having a month of major pitching and promoting, it helps if I feel more resourceful before I begin. I do this by recalling the fact that I know how to do pitching and promoting. I've done it before on previous occasions – it has sometimes been easy and at other times hard. I get results about 50% of the time and I've always had enough work over the last two decades. So it seems that events generally work out from my pitching experiences – that's encouraging. This recall is like tapping into my memory bank of successes.

Once you do that, you can ask yourself if you are willing to keep going – resilience is often something that we choose. The answer may also give you extra strength.

If you want a more structured way to tap into your reservoir of successful determination, try these questions:

TECHNIQUES

Determination and memory

Set up: Take ten minutes and reflect on these questions to tap into determination and persistence:

- What was the best experience I've had of being determined at work or in life in the past? Recall it as clearly as possible: What was I thinking, feeling and doing?
- What went well on this occasion?
- What did I do to make that good result happen?
- What's my learning from this about persistence and determination?
- What are two small steps I could take now, to increase my determination and staying power?
- How willing am I to stay determined and carry out those steps?
- When will I carry out those steps?

TECHNIQUES

Resilience and memory

You can do a variation of the technique above for more general resilience. For example, reflecting on:

- What was the best experience I've had of being resilient in the past? Recall it as clearly as possible: What was I thinking, feeling and doing?
- What went well on this occasion?
- What did I do to make that good result happen?
- What's my learning from this about resilience?
- What are two small steps I could take now, to increase my resilience?
- How willing am I to stay determined and carry out those steps? When will I carry out those steps?

Tapping into a more useful mindset like this via memories is an emotional intelligence skill. It helps us be more resourceful and resilient by boosting our self-esteem before action in an evidence-based way.

Saying 'no' and it's time to go

There may be times when you simply need to learn to say no, to have boundaries or even to leave. Let's begin with no: no to more work, no to more or less responsibility, no to a project that compromises your values, no to a deadline.

Often with coaching clients when exploring being resilient to others' expectations, I begin with the basics, learning to say no 'in big and small ways'. This sometimes involves a goal of managing upwards, peers and other staff. Discussing your concerns and saying no, being resilient to people aiming to persuade you, can be tough and may involve some anxiety. For example: 'What would happen if I say no to peers, to senior staff, to customers, to external partners?' 'What would happen if I said no to my mentor/mentee?'

These are the dialogues and role-plays that we practise in coaching. They help you to understand where and when you needed to give reasons for pushing back, and where and when you don't. A focused coaching conversation also helps you see where you need to stand your ground more and be less willing to give in, and how to come across as more authentic because you believe in yourself and your right to say no.

Whenever I have worked with coachees around standing up for themselves, fantastic things happen. They stay in their jobs and flourish, or they leave their jobs and find something new, wonderful and more humane. This is a huge area of learning, and sometimes as you learn to set new boundaries, you can feel odd, guilty even. So my recommendation here is to work with a coach or mentor. A coach will help you find your own solutions, role-play and support you. An experienced mentor will offer you insights on what they have done to stand up for themselves.

TECHNIQUES

Saying no to too much work, deadlines or responsibility

If you're not in coaching at the moment, it's still possible to learn the resilience skill of saying no.

- Reflect on the benefits of saying no at work – what would it give you in the short term and long term?
- Explore how you feel about saying no to various people – teams, managers, clients and partners.
- Explore what kinds of no there are. For example, could you say, 'No, I'm not going to do that extensive piece of research, but I'll do a smaller amount'? Could you say no to a deadline and ask for an extension? Could you simply say, 'No, I've got too much on my plate'?
- Until you find a coach or mentor, practise saying no in smaller, less charged situations, in circumstances which are less challenging for you. That way you can start kindly and gradually learning to say no, until you get more professional support or feel more confident.

Time to go?

A final note: sometimes you are 'pushing back', managing up and it works – it's really powerful and you get a good result. But sometimes it just doesn't seem to shift the challenge, or the action you took doesn't seem like the right move. Perhaps it's perceived as too assertive, or the situation is too charged, or your employer simply doesn't care enough to take on board your feedback. A participant on a recent workshop[42] reminded me that your resilience is fine if you are stretching and challenging yourself, but not if you're mentally taking the stress home with you. If it starts to affect your home life and your wider well-being, it's time to reconsider how long you can continue to stretch yourself.

Some time ago, I encountered a difficult and bullying line manager. I tried all different kinds of strategies – negotiating, deep listening, working on my mindset. Things would occasionally improve temporarily, but it was still stressful. My resilience was being stretched and I felt that, although it wasn't affecting my home life, it was affecting how I felt about work. I didn't feel confident enough to go to HR. I was new to working in this organisation and I noticed that another staff member who formally complained – we were both on temporary contracts – didn't get their contract renewed. This may have been a coincidence, but it left me feeling nervous – I wasn't doing evidence-based 'reality thinking' at the time.

As time progressed, the bullying began to affect my emotional and psychological well-being and cause me an immense amount of stress. Previously a deeply motivated and dynamic person, I was now losing my confidence at work. I reached the point where I decided that I would quit. It was a stressful, but good decision, that I thought would help my well-being. I felt resilient enough to make that decision, a decision that I felt would enable me to rebuild my resilience, perhaps elsewhere in another role with an easier line manager. It was a shift that completely suited me in many ways, and I flourished from that day. (Looking back on the situation, I now believe it would have been worth speaking with HR informally, pursuing a complaint and maybe even considering a disciplinary process, or later down the line, complaining formally via a union representative, but this all comes from the benefit of experience that I didn't have at the time.)

TECHNIQUES

You've reached your limit – is it time to go?

There are a few different techniques here, rather than one detailed one. In the situation where you feel you are under huge pressure and it is starting to seep into your home life and affect your well-being, you might:

- Read Chapter 2 and identify if you need to attend to your well-being. Then take some small steps for change.
- Read the list about employer responsibility (found in the Introduction) and reflect on what kind of employer you have at present.
- Explore if collective problem solving or collective bargaining is the right way to bring about the change that you want. Being resilient within a group or team can be powerful. Read Chapter 5: Let's All Work Together for more teamwork resilience building approaches.
- Explore if you truly feel it is time to leave your job and also if it's financially possible to do that. In my opinion, no job is worth my well-being at the end of the day. We are all more than our jobs, our roles and the part we play in an organisation. Revise Chapter 3: Changing Mindsets and the section on 'learning the lesson' to help you gain some perspective.

There are many considerations here and only you know what's right. From a resilience perspective, it's worth noting that by saying 'I've had enough: it's time to go' you are also making a resilient decision, rather than enabling a fragility or weakness. But tread carefully and perhaps see a career coach first.

Tips: Launch

For shifting 'stuckness':

- Use Solutions-Focused methods to help you find small steps for change.
- Learn to relax, using the 'Inner Smile', so you can tap into your intuition before deciding on actions.

For learning flexibility:

- Reflect on the compromise questions, really noticing what you feel and seeing if you can move to a more flexible mindset.

For staying power:

- Take a break and see if it reenergises you to get going again. Rest if you need and reapply the Five Ways of Well-Being.
- Tap into your memory bank of past 'staying power' successes.
- Connect with a coach or mentor to support you in learning to say 'no'. Practise saying no in small ways at work.
- Find yourself some support for any 'It's time to go' exploration. This might involve attending to your well-being, collaborative support, or using coaching or mentoring.

5: Let's All Work Together

Are you:

- **Feeling that you have run out of steam, because you've been doing *all* the thinking and carrying out *all* the actions?**
- **Finding your solo resilience-building actions are not having the impact that you hoped for?**
- **Facing a larger challenge, that might benefit from an inspired and collaborative group tackling it together?**
- **Simply feeling like you'd like to be more of a team player?**

If this sounds like you, it might be beneficial to build your personal resilience with peers, or in a group. So far in this book we have focused a great deal on techniques that you can use personally to build your resilience. That's great in many ways: it strengthens your emotional intelligence, can really develop your inner resilience and gives you a strong sense of independence. But sometimes, if you are tired of behaving like a superhero, using up your reserves of energy, risking burnout, or just needing to take part in more team work, you can explore building resilience with people and with a network, rather than alone.

Working with a peer, in a group or with co-working colleagues to build your resilience, you may experience:

- Solving challenges more easily as you and a group pull together
- Feeling more supported as you become more resilient

- Feeling less isolated at work around new challenges, new changes and an 'innovation culture'
- Feeling part of a stronger co-working community
- Better and more enjoyable relationships at work
- Feeling more energised and less close to burnout
- More effective and democratic teamwork

In this chapter we will look at collaboration, the benefits from working with other people and some collaborative resilience-building techniques, including reflecting on collaboration opportunities, peer coaching using TGROW, resilience mapping and professional coaching.

A successful collaboration story

Three years ago, after a challenging time at work and in my wider life, I was feeling pessimistic and somewhat cynical. This is when my colleague inspired me to take part in a Massive Open Online Course created by Massachusetts Institute of Technology (MIT)[43]. The aim of the programme was to help participants collaboratively tackle local and national challenges. A group of participants decided during the programme, to set up a local leadership school in Brixton, South London. Our aim was to empower others to learn how to collaboratively bring about community change and tackle tough local challenges. We focused on one of the biggest issues in our borough – the food system and food poverty. It was no easy task; we hoped to at least build a stronger network of people working in the food system. At best, we aimed to launch some projects that might combat food poverty, or tackle food waste in our borough.

As our leadership school project blossomed, I found myself involved in a substantial programme development process. I was designing and co-facilitating an eight-week programme, with what emerged as my dream coordination and facilitation team. My previous cynicism and pessimism took an about turn as, as part of my learning, I discovered projects all over the world tacking injustice, inequality, and tales of personal and community development. As time went on, the leadership school project became the most exciting working experience of my year.

I felt truly resilient as I:

- Worked long hours with my inspiring team and yet didn't feel exhausted – I felt dynamic and re-energised
- Pushed through my small upsets about group dynamics and found synergy and flexibility in my communication and in my general work approach
- Noticed that my cynicism about the world of work had disappeared
- Rediscovered my joy in everyday work activities

Practical successes of collaborative work

As the first programme in our leadership school, the group and I launched a 'Grow Your Own Leaders' programme. The launch was an overwhelming success – the twenty-five places were immediately booked up within a few hours of going live. The programme was filled with interactive activities: from mapping exercises (see my version below) to mindfulness, team coaching circles, journaling and even Social Presencing Theatre – a type of mindful movement process to help you see a system more clearly, such as the system of inequality or education. We immersed ourselves in both learning and facilitating. The participant group tackled food poverty and food waste, by setting up London's first Community Fridge[44], setting up an estate fence-growing vegetable garden and a community-led café.

The programme snowballed, attracting a lot of attention, and we carried out a live stream with presentations to over 15,000 people. I was involved in the early stages of crowdfunding and launching The Community Fridge – named 'Freddie the Fridge', a fridge with free food that is donated by cafés, restaurants and local people.

Our innovative little project was featured in the London newspaper, the *Evening Standard*. It was also featured in major UK newspapers, as food poverty in the UK became an increasing discussion point and began to receive the exposure it needed as a national urgent challenge. The well-known chef, Jamie Oliver, came and filmed us, as he planned to launch a community fridge in another area of the country. Amazingly, people from all over the world came to see Freddie!

In our small way, we were making a difference. The programme raised awareness of how community fridges, community cafés, and estate food-growing projects could make a contribution to help food poverty and prevent food waste.

All this only came about because our team were communicating effectively, tuning into their inspiration and facing a local challenge with courage. The team were a delight to work and learn with. On the smaller sub-facilitation team, I also knew I was collaborating with some incredibly talented people, on a meaningful leadership project. Gradually, I noticed I was more energised, resourceful and generally feeling more resilient. My enthusiasm for life was back. My dark gloom and cynicism had disappeared.

For me, the insight from this experience is clear: seek out and take part in meaningful collaborative projects with people with whom you enjoy working. In your team, take part in innovative learning activities, such as peer coaching, team coaching or mapping exercises to inspire you to collaboratively tackle challenges. During the programme, both facilitators and participants mapped out topics and systems (e.g. the food system) so we could have a clearer perspective on potential obstacles. This way we could see connections, resources and possible solutions. We also used team coaching and peer coaching for reflection, digging deep for insights and for clarity.

TECHNIQUES

Reflecting on collaboration opportunities

Set up: This is easy to do anywhere quiet. You need five to ten minutes.

Activity: Consider what you might want from a workplace collaboration project. Identify some qualities, e.g. tackling X issue, enjoying the teamwork, trying out new activities, or getting a pilot launched.

Examine your working life and see if there are any emerging opportunities for collaboration: projects, tasks or groups. What's on the horizon? Consider: what, where, who with, how and why might you take part? If there is a new project connected with your work in some way, how might you contribute to it? What skills could you provide? Who's involved and what is your dynamic with them like? Is it something you'd like to get involved with? Does it make you smile when you think about it? If you haven't yet been invited to take part, see if you can create a business case for you to be involved.

Peer Coaching and TGROW

Peer Coaching is an approach where you and a colleague are 'coaches' for each other in one or a series of conversations. The essence of Peer Coaching is that you and your colleague find solutions to a workplace challenge you each have, using listening, feedback and questions. It's a supportive way to enable you both to reflect, in a safe supportive space and without giving advice. Instead you use:

- Listening skills
- Curiosity and open questions
- Feedback on what you have heard

Critically, you allow the other person who is being asked the questions to find their own solutions *without your guidance.*

There are many models you can use to help you structure a peer coaching conversation, but for ease I like the TGROW[45]. The original GROW model (GOAL, REALITY, OPTIONS, WILL) was created and popularised in the 1980s by Graham Alexander, Alan Fine and Sir John Whitmore, before Miles Downey adapted it into TGROW (the added T stands for Topic). It is a popular model in Professional Coaching and Life Coaching, and forms a useful framework for a Peer Coaching conversation.

TECHNIQUES

Peer Coaching with TGROW

This is a resilience-building technique that can enhance workplace relationships and get you working collaboratively with peers to find solutions. It can also improve your experience of supporting your colleagues, without giving solutions.

Find a colleague or peer in your co-working space whom you trust to be discreet and a good listener, and ask them if they would like to practise peer coaching to address individual workplace challenges.

> Aim: You'll get to address one personal challenge each, and you'll take it in turns to be coach and coachee. You'll have fifteen to twenty minutes each way, with one person being coach and the other coachee and then swapping, using the TGROW coaching model questions.

Your roles as peer coaches are to enable each person in turn to find their own answers to the issue, challenge or goal they are discussing. Collaboration here means working together to find the solution through listening, but not advice giving. The coach asks questions and listens deeply, while the coachee listens to the questions, reflects deeply and answers out loud. The coachee might make some brief notes after each answer, if they like. Allow time for the coachee to answer the questions, but keep things on track with the timing, so that there is a regular flow to proceedings.

Stick to the focus of the questions. Coaches should avoid going off on a tangent or asking different questions. You might not need to ask all the questions, but you could ask questions from each section in the TGROW order. When the coachee has discussed the final answer, you pause, make any notes and swap over roles – so coach becomes coachee and vice versa. Then the new coachee brings their topic to the discussion.

TGROW model questions:

TOPIC: Initial Clarification

- What would you like to think/talk about?
- What would you like to focus on?
- Tell me about...

Establish the GOAL for the conversation and longer term too

- What would you like to take from this conversation?
- What would you like to know, or be able to do by the time we complete this conversation?
- What is the goal for this conversation?
- What do you want to achieve? (This is the bigger goal, not the goal for the conversation.)
- What would achieving this lead to in the long term?
- How would this benefit you?

Examine current REALITY

- What is the current position (e.g. with this goal or issue)?
- What have you done so far?
- What progress have you made?
- What has worked well so far? What did you do to make that happen?
- When have things been better?
- Describe your thoughts about that person/situation.
- What, who, when, how often?
- What is the effect or result of that?

Explore the OPTIONS

- What are your options at present?
- What options are there from your past successes?
- How could your learning from your past successes help you to move forward?
- What could you do?
- What else could you do? And what else?
- What if this or that constraint were removed?
- What are the benefits and downsides of each option?
- What will be the first signs of that working successfully? What successful signs will you notice? What will others notice?

Establish the WILL

- What will you do?
- What will be the first step you will take?
- When will you do that?
- What could stop you moving forward?
- And how will you overcome it?

So find a colleague, identify a topic each for discussion and find a confidential space to speak over a hot drink. Trust me: peer coaching is supportive, fun and even positively addictive.

With a little practice, you can deepen the coach's role by building on the listening and feedback skills:

- Listen deeply, with empathy to the words and meaning.
- Occasionally give observation-based feedback about what you're hearing, e.g. 'I hear you saying…' or your interpretation, e.g. 'I think this means you feel…'
- Avoid giving your own opinions or advice as coach, e.g. 'It sounds like you might want to try…'

Over time, if you continue with the same person, you and your peer coach could also have more general discussions, such as discussing the REALLY RESILIENT visualisation and the NOT-REALLY RESILIENT features list.

Resilience mapping

Have you ever experienced a whole team feeling 'stuck' when facing a challenge? Perhaps they perceive it as a problem, rather than a goal? Or perhaps you have been trying to solve something on your own, which could potentially be solved as a group or team? All these experiences to some extent are filled with 'stuckness' and isolation that makes them useful areas of focus for Resilience Mapping.

I created this Resilience Mapping activity five years ago, inspired by Relationship Mapping, a visual process to help you see relationships more clearly. Resilience Mapping gives you a whole new perspective. It enables you to step back and see relationships, resources or networks you have built in the workplace, around a particular theme or goal or challenge. It's a tool that supports you to pinpoint the relationship/network gaps, and identify how to make the most of your resources to help tackle a particular issue. Doing Resilience Mapping as a team strengthens your teamwork and highlights how your stronger network helps you all.

TECHNIQUES

Resilience Mapping

Set up: Gather your team together. You need be willing to facilitate a bit (guide, support, make sure everyone gets to contribute, keep it on track and manage timings).

Activity:

A. About a week in advance:

Invite a group of four to seven colleagues or peers to take part in a Resilience Mapping activity, to help you all find a way forward with a current work challenge or goal, with the aim of increasing resilience. If you work in a co-working space, you might want to do this with peers, choosing a topic which is relevant to a few entrepreneurs, e.g. marketing, productivity, handling tough projects, etc.

Invite ideas and give suggestions for the topic or challenge to be discussed, identifying what you want to be more resilient to, e.g. team resilience to funding cuts, resilience to increasing customer expectations, etc. See if you can agree the topic to be discussed in advance to save time.

Explain to the group that on the day of the Mapping Activity, you will meet for about sixty to ninety minutes. Explain they won't need to prepare anything, but request that on the day they be willing to share ideas and take part in the discussion. Let them know you'll facilitate to keep it on track and on time.

Choose a suitable room for the activity, that is nice for group work (e.g. with a window and good light). Make sure there are enough tables and chairs, two flip chart sheets, varied colour marker pens and highlighter pens.

B. On the day:

Arrange the room with a small group of desks café-style (grouped together, surrounded by chairs).

- Place a sheet of A1 flip chart paper on the table with pens and marker pens spread around.

- Invite people to sit or stand round the table, and explain how you will guide them through each stage of mapping. Ask if there are any quick questions before you start.
- Restate the topic: what you want to be resilient to. Write this in the middle of the flip chart, surrounded by a circle.
- Lead a five to ten-minute discussion on what has helped you resolve this issue so far, e.g. people, places and resources. Aim to get everyone to contribute without putting anyone on the spot.
- Explain you will now co-create a spidergram (with the issue in the middle of the page), surrounded by key words that map out these resources. Include anyone or anything that has helped you solve the problem so far. For example, maybe books are a resource, or a certain website, a group, a person/staff member/ other stakeholder who has offered insights or support. See if there are a few people who will scribe the ideas into a clear spidergram or invite the entire group to co-create it, using the flip chart markers. You should aim to end up with between six and ten resources between you.
- Keep adding information, asking the group to identify the people, places and resources that you might connect with and make use of in the future, even if you have no connection to them yet. Here's one I created when my company website crashed and was unrecoverable. I wanted to be resilient to negative impacts on my business, e.g. potential clients not seeing a live website and therefore losing work.

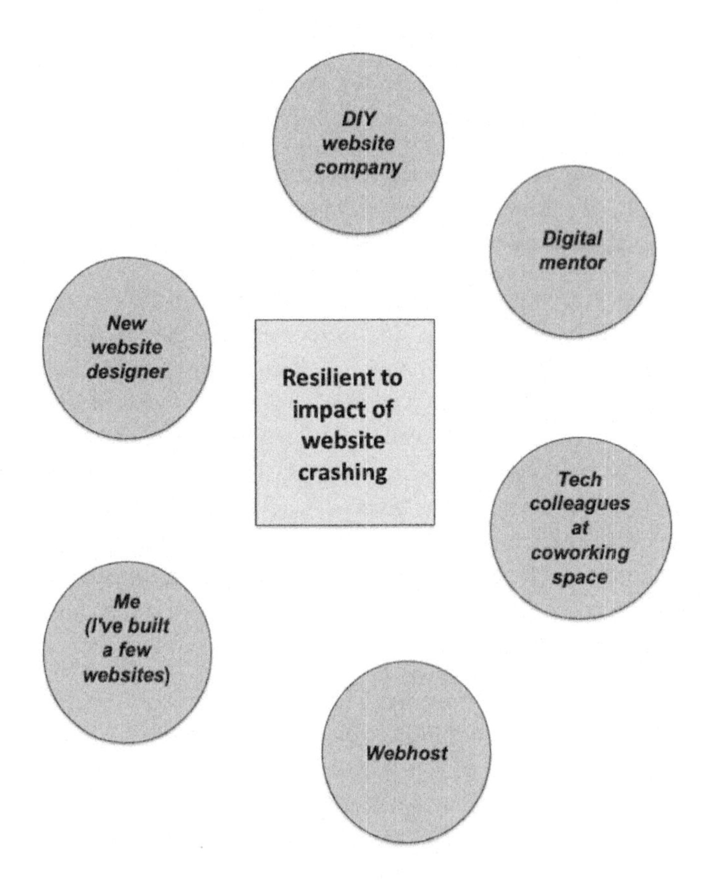

C. Next steps: Assessment of relationship

Explain to the group that, using the highlighter pens, you will now add in a relationship key, connecting each resource to the centre, like branches.

Use this key:

- Branch with thick lines = good relationship or resources that you use well
- Branch with one line = new relationship
- No lines = no relationship or conflict or difficulty

Also, you could work with colours so that the relationship lines are easier to see.

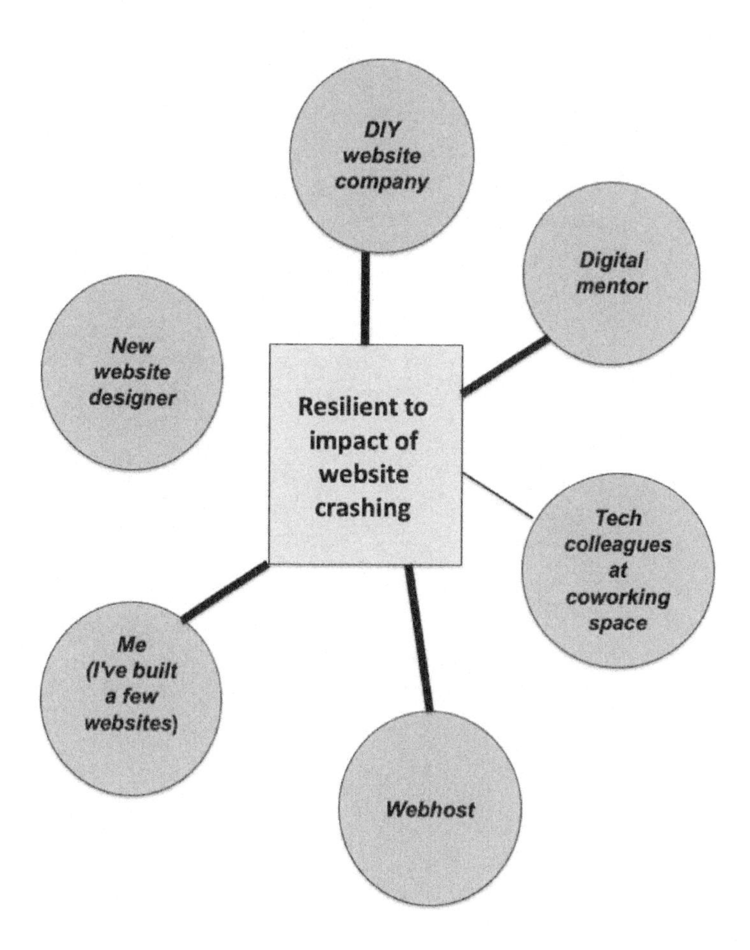

D. Now discuss and add in to the sheet a 'get and give' for each resource. This is what you get from each relationship, and this is what you give to each relationship. For example, in my version I give money to my web host and in return I get a hosting service. Here's the beginning of my get and give:

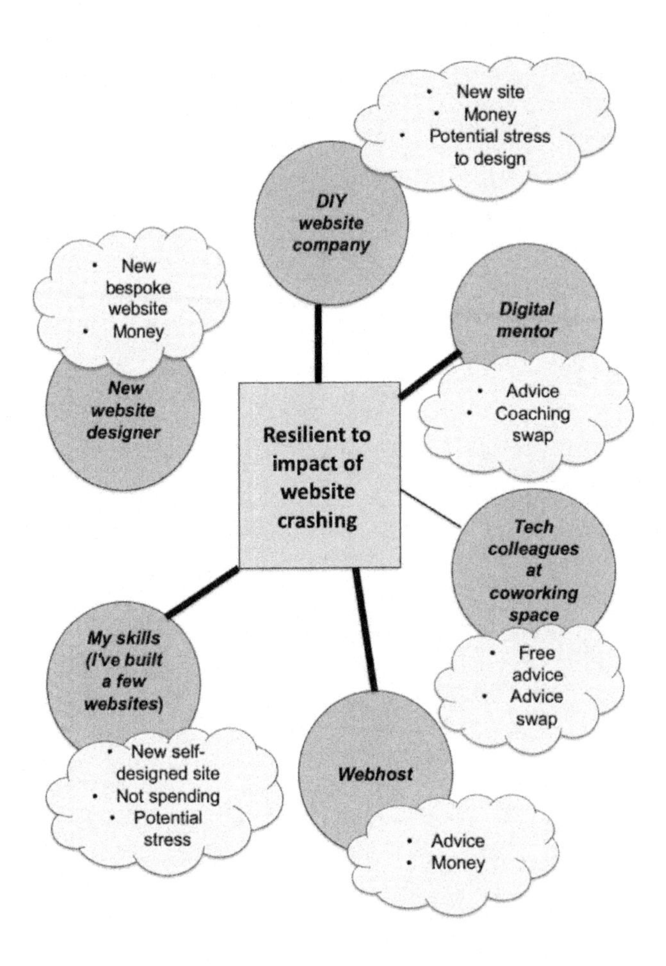

E. As a group, discuss which three resources seem best from those listed to help you tackle the current issue. Number them 1, 2 and 3. Here's my version (I've removed some of the other resources to give you a clearer picture):

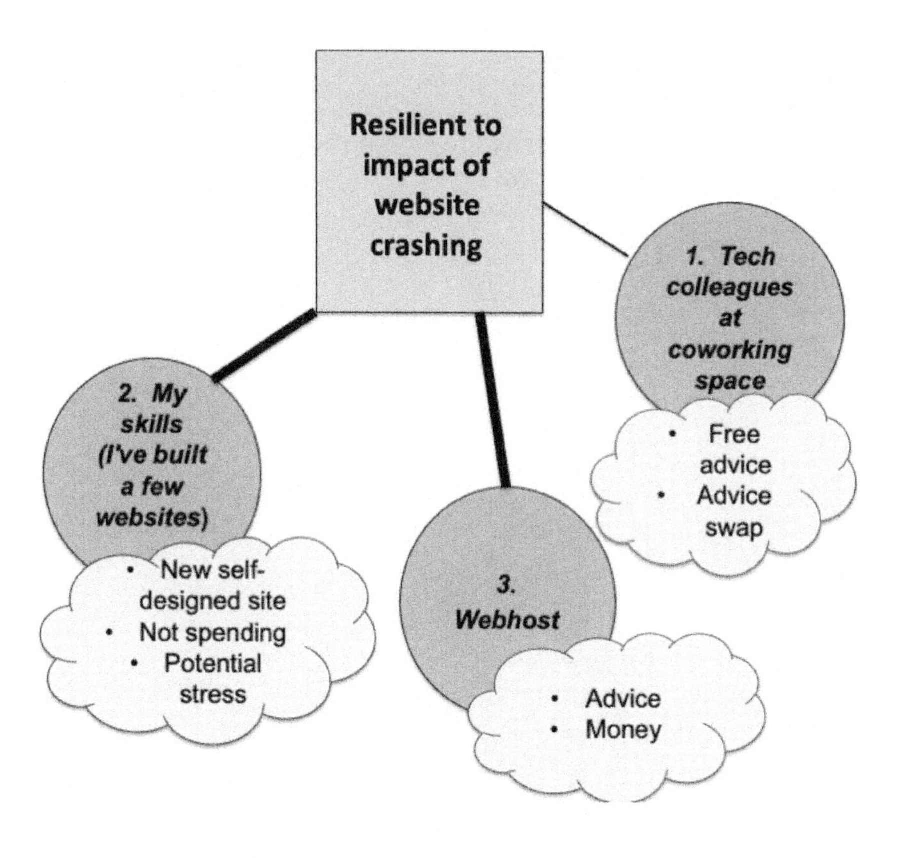

F. Discuss and add in small steps/actions you could take connected with those three resources. They can be random steps, collaborative and not necessarily in order (e.g. if a particular website is listed as your best resource, you could agree to research it between you later in the week). Agree who will do what and when, and at which point you will reconnect to discuss.

What to do	When
1. Discuss with co-working colleagues. (This led me to another action not on the list – a new DIY design website company using a much easier design service than the one I had used in the past.)	Tomorrow
2. Reflect on my skills and stress levels. (This helped me identify I could do an easy DIY website in a day, but not a complex one.)	After speaking to colleagues and webhost
3. Speak with webhost about steps for resolving the issue. (This helped me with some tech stuff, financial decisions and also my confidence around resolving this.)	Today

G. Finally, ask the group to review the activity with you: what worked and what could you amend or improve if you use it another time?

Professional coaching to support your resilience

Ten years ago, I was working in an organisation as a senior lecturer, doing a job that I enjoyed, with colleagues whom I appreciated. Slowly, I began to realise I'd been there for too long. I was finding it harder, as I was also freelancing part-time in another organisation as a teacher trainer and teacher, but being your own boss is an amazing freedom that is hard to replicate in a salaried role.

The beginning of the financial crisis kicked in and I lost my senior lecturer job. Within six weeks, I also lost my other part-time job. Losing both jobs was a shock and I lost my voice for a week after I heard the news. Fortunately, I negotiated for career coaching as part of my leaving package. I already knew from some previous coaching that top of the list of my career values were 'freedom' and 'doing work I really enjoy'. When one of the organisations that had given me the redundancy notice offered me a new role – something I had little interest in – I knew it didn't meet my values.

In the first session, I sat with my career coach and mapped out all my networks of contacts, potential clients and sources of possible interesting work. My map looked full; it looked like I could make a living from coaching and freelance facilitation. I decided to turn down the unsuitable job offer and go my own way.

It was a rocky start and as the financial crisis progressed, I lost all my clients within the first year, as they were mainly government quangos that all closed down. What a year! However, ten years later, I'm still doing that work and so much more, having added keynote speeches and consultancy to my work. I love my job, working with many staff, leaders, managers and organisations. I also love being my own line manager. About five years into my journey and when I felt the need to do so, I got a part-time salaried job of six hours a week. I wouldn't rule that out if need be – it's good to be flexible. Most of all, I am now doing what I want and I have my work freedom – which was top of my values list.

Sometimes you need a coach or mentor to help you see 'the wood for the trees' and to help you feel you can make the best decisions in a crisis situation. Sometimes it gives you a bird's eye view. It can be useful to work in this collaborative way and less in isolation. It also gives you another encouraging professional to do your Resilience Mapping activity with.

Some additional resilience-building tips related to connections

1. Make and deepen your individual connections with people in your organisation and in your sector. Good relationships with colleagues are so important. Don't underestimate this. Good workplace relationships can take time to build. Explore where you can ask for and receive support about resilience to change and challenge from those more established relationships.

Enhance existing workplace relationships by *really listening* and finding out more about your colleagues and their role in your organisation. If you know them well and trust them, ask for and receive constructive feedback on how you could be more resilient to change or challenge. Having constructive feedback can strengthen your resilience.

2. Evidence shows us that having and making use of strong relationships builds resilience. Make group connections and join or attend networks. Larger organisations may have various forums for research staff, tech staff, managers, directors, departmental administrators and office support staff. You could look for a specialist group, like a women's or men's group, or a BAME group.

Some people find that being active in networks and other specialist groups provides social and career support and can help with preparing you for the future (a key resilience skill). You can discuss challenges and goals at meetings and therefore feel less isolated.

3. If you like the idea of belonging to a workplace union to help you collectively negotiate for change, seek out your local union representative. For a small annual fee, you could feel more resilient by belonging to a group with shared values and goals who may help to stand up for your workplace rights. You may find that you get access to practical advice and support during times of challenge and change.

4. Ask for a coach or mentor to work with you in your organisation, or perhaps find someone more skilled and knowledgeable and ask if they would mentor you. Consider in advance what you want to learn from a mentor about resilience. A mentor's role is to share their expertise, or help you find your own inner expertise – all of which can help you build resilience. If you can't find a mentor within your organisation, seek a mentor outside of it. Mentoring is generally a free service.

Coaching may be available with an internal staff coach, or sometimes with an external coach. External coaches help you discover your own ideas for how to build inner resilience, tending to share less of their own resilience expertise. They use a focused style of non-judgemental open conversation, with questions and feedback. External coaching is generally a paid service and is usually organised by HR or Learning and Development departments.

Summary Tips: collaboration, teams and peer coaching

- Seek out and take part in collaborative projects with colleagues to tackle tough challenges.
- Speak with a colleague you have a good relationship with. Enquire if they know about peer coaching. If appropriate, have a discussion with them about what peer coaching is and the benefits. Ask them if they'd be interested in meeting with you for peer coaching over a tea or coffee. You could meet face to face or online.
- Try some mapping techniques during the process of working on a project or to tackle an unmet goal. Get your group together and try out mapping a shared challenge.

Conclusion: Resilience Takeaways

There is much you can do both individually and with others to improve your resilience in your working life, to be REALLY RESILIENT. Some resilience-building moments are fun, while others feel like hard, gruelling work. As I look at it, I've survived losing two jobs, setting up a business, losing all my clients, some challenging physical health issues and maintaining a healthy working life in the middle of a recession, a global financial crisis and the craziness of lockdown. Some tough experiences, but some new opportunities to grasp, as well.

As you continue on your resilience-building journey, treat it as a learning opportunity – picture yourself at the school of being REALLY RESILIENT at work, growing, becoming stronger and even *embracing* change. Keep going, keep flexing, attend to your well-being and rest when you need to.

In time, you'll feel stronger, more empowered and you'll have memories of having been flexible, adaptable and persistent, all while overcoming obstacles. You'll have that inner confidence that you can handle almost any challenge, change, innovation request or unexpected upset.

Most of all remind yourself, as you keep learning resilience, there will be a day when you shift from surviving to thriving at work. You'll know that whatever may come your way, you'll cope and find ways to flourish.

You'll become REALLY RESILIENT.

Acknowledgements

Thank you to my wonderful mum – for being you and your big heart. I love you.

Thank you to my lovely husband, Ray, for being there with me whilst I learnt and continue to learn to be more resilient at work and in life. For your humour, strength, love and laughter.

Thank you to my lovely family and to my lovely other mum, Josephine McFarlane.

Thank you to Nanette for twenty-seven years of insight, wisdom and encouragement to write over those years, and for introducing me to, or constantly reminding me of, some of the most amazing techniques here: curiosity thinking, possibility thinking, relaxation, being present and mindful and resilient. You are a shining star.

Thank you to my colleagues and friends, Miranda and Penny, for many years of our work together, conversations, facilitation, encouragement and friendship.

Thanks to my editor, Bryony Sutherland, for sharp, insightful editing and laughter. Thanks to Caroline Goldsmith, my creative designer. Thanks to Janie for my amazing portrait photos.

Thanks to Janice for a memorable coaching mind-mapping session - just at the perfect time .

Thanks to all my friends who read a chapter or blurb early on and gave me encouraging feedback: Barbara, Wayne Murray, Miranda, Janie, Kim, Dawn, Kirsty, Roy and Jeannie. Thanks to Andy Matheson and Eve Turner for linking me with the right people to get this book edited, designed and published.

Thank you to Rebecca Henry-Litteck, Fiona Evans, Nichola Stallwood, Theresa Mellon, Claire Collins, Eve Turner, Karl Daly, Shaun Lincoln, Emma Mason, John Vorhaus, Gerald Jones, Joannie

Andrews, Ian Ashman, Khalid Joomaye, Karl Daly, Nyree Grierson, Jenny Garratt, Jackee Holder, Urmi Joshi, Joanne Miles, Emma Brown, staff at BIAZA and EAZA and staff at Skyros Centre and many others for giving me opportunities to train, coach and learn.

Thanks to Michelle Halse for endless conversations about digital courses, work, planning and value.

Thank you to Kyle (B Street Digital) for finally getting me writing, getting me publishing and generally for inspiring me over a year to believe this could all happen. Thank you to Antoinette Johnson for getting me writing and dealing with my perfectionist self. Thank you to Phillip Weeks for encouraging me to write and helping me stay healthy. Thank you to Leonie Abrahamson, Jackee Holder and Gerald Jones for encouraging me to write.

Thank you to all my supportive reviewers for your kind testimonials.

Thank you to all my lovely coachees and workshop participants over twenty-nine years for helping me feel fulfilled by my work.

Team hug and thanks to everyone at Impact Brixton for providing the best community co-working space, for Wednesday cakes, Friday lunch and being the perfect place for writing.

Love and thanks to all my friends, including the Chicken Skins, Noor, Camillo, Frankie, Elena, Janie, Kirsty, Barbara, Anna, Michelle, Sarah Natalia and Vanessa. For fun, love, thousands of conversations, laughter and friendship.

About the Author

Andry Anastasis McFarlane (aka Andry Anastasiou) is a qualified and experienced executive and management coach, a learning consultant, a facilitator and a keynote speaker.

Andry has worked with organisations for over twenty years, supporting them to improve staff and team performance, well-being, enhance communication and develop successful managers, leaders staff and teams. Her client list includes ZSL London Zoo, Notting Hill Housing Trust, previously An Office of the Deputy Prime-Minister, St George's University of London, London School of Tropical Medicine and Hygiene, Federal Libraries Group and Friends of the Earth.

Andry has researched and practised well-being for twenty-six years. She originally trained as an auricular acupuncturist and reflexologist and worked in the NHS (voluntary role), HIV care and in seven substance-abuse clinics in London.

Andry is a full member of the Association for Coaching (MAC). She is qualified with ILM as a coach and mentor, and is a qualified teacher with a PGCE from the Institute of Education. When she isn't leading workshops or coaching, she spends her time gardening, walking and working hard not to be the worst mosaic artist ever.

Contact Andry and Continue Your Learning

Keep Learning with Andry's Programmes for Individuals, Staff and Organisations

In the UK, Andry offers executive coaching, workshops and courses under the trading name The Learning Moment. Andry's learning programmes also help develop well-being, management and leadership, coaching and mentoring skills for your staff and yourself.

For individuals and organisations who want to master their resilience skills and progress with added support, you can deepen your experience of building resilience with Andry's online and face-to-face courses, resilience coaching, and resilience videos. You can also access a free REALLY RESILIENT GUIDE introductory programme.

For more information on all programmes, including free online courses, please visit thelearningmoment.org

Register for any REALLY RESILIENT GUIDE online programme and you'll gain access to the Facebook community learning group, where you can ask questions. Search Facebook @thelearningmoment.

For enquires about Andry working with your organisation or with yourself, please get in touch at andry@thelearningmoment.org

You'll also find Andry blogging on LinkedIn.

On Twitter, you can stay updated with her UK work @_learningmoment.

Get the latest books and resilience news

To join Andry's mailing list for free online courses, news and resilience tips, visit www.thelearningmoment.org

To purchase more copies

I'm an efficient but lazy present buyer: when I find one good book, I buy it for various different friends' birthdays. Hopefully you've had a wonderful read and you'll be thinking, 'This is the perfect present for all my friends and colleagues.' For more copies, please visit Amazon and you can buy the Kindle version.

Reviews

Please feed me – I get hungry for feedback! If you have found the book useful, please leave a review on Amazon.

Endnotes

[1] Thanks to Ray McFarlane for coining this term by talking with me about a series of 'life experiments' he has taken over the years.

[2] https://dictionary.cambridge.org/dictionary/english/adaptability (accessed November 2019)

[3] https://carolepemberton.co.uk/resilience-questionnaire/

[4] Goleman, Daniel (1995) *Emotional Intelligence: Why It Can Matter More Than IQ*. Bantam Books, first edition

[5] https://www.gov.uk/government/collections/mental-capital-and-wellbeing (accessed November 2019). See various reports including '5 Ways to Mental Wellbeing' and also details on the research project leading up to the '5 Ways of Wellbeing'.

[6] https://www.standard.co.uk/lifestyle/esmagazine/equinox-hotel-new-york-fitness-a4107496.html (accessed November 2019)

[7] https://www.independent.co.uk/life-style/health-and-families/self-deprecating-humour-greater-psychological-wellbeing-link-study-university-of-granada-spain-a8207976.html (accessed November 2019)

[8] https://www.forbes.com/sites/victoriaforster/2019/06/13/scientists-have-worked-out-the-optimal-dose-of-nature-required-for-good-health-and-wellbeing/ (accessed November 2019)

[9] https://www.theguardian.com/lifeandstyle/2019/jun/10/i-started-mentoring-young-people-and-gave-my-own-life-a-purpose (accessed November 2019)

[10] https://neweconomics.org/2008/10/five-ways-to-wellbeing-the-evidence/ (accessed November 2019)

[11] https://www.mentalhealth.org.nz/assets/5-ways-toolkit/Five-Ways-to-Wellbeing-at-Worknew.pdf (accessed November 2019)

[12] https://www.facebook.com/makerhood/ (accessed November 2019)

[13] 'Making Uncovered', a beautiful five-minute documentary by my husband filmmaker, Ray McFarlane: https://vimeo.com/72914334 (accessed November 2019)

[14] https://www.mentalhealth.org.nz/assets/5-ways-toolkit/Five-Ways-to-Wellbeing-at-Worknew.pdf (accessed November 2019)

[15] http://www.bell-project.eu/cms/ (accessed October 2019)

[16] Dr, Dispenza, Joe (2014) *You are the Placebo*. Hay House Inc., USA, first edition

[17] https://www.mentalhealth.org.nz/assets/5-ways-toolkit/Five-Ways-to-Wellbeing-at-Worknew.pdf (accessed November 2019)

18 Lathia N, Sandstrom GM, Mascolo C, Rentfrow PJ (2017) *Happier People Live More Active Lives: Using Smartphones to Link Happiness and Physical Activity.* Available at https://doi.org/10.1371/journal.pone.0160589 (accessed October 2019)

[19] Penedo FJ Dahn JR. *Exercise and well-being: a review of mental and physical health benefits associated with physical activity.* Current Opinion in Psychiatry. 2005; 18(2): 189–193.

[20] Some of these symptoms can be signs of menopause or perimenopause, which would be appropriate for my age. I advise female readers experiencing similar symptoms to also consult their GP.

[21] www.bluezones.com (accessed November 2019)

[22] https://www.mentalhealth.org.nz/assets/5-ways-toolkit/Five-Ways-to-Wellbeing-at-Worknew.pdf (accessed November 2019)

[23] Emmons, Robert A. and McCullough, Michael E. *Counting Blessings Versus Burdens: An Experimental Investigation of Gratitude and Subjective Well-Being in Daily Life.* Journal of Personality and Social Psychology 2003 Vol. 84, No. 2, 377–389. https://greatergood.berkeley.edu/images/application_uploads/Emmons-CountingBlessings.pdf (accessed November 2019)

[24] https://www.mentalhealth.org.nz/assets/5-ways-toolkit/Five-Ways-to-Wellbeing-at-Worknew.pdf (accessed November 2019)

[25] https://www.medicalnewstoday.com/articles/318406.php (accessed October 2019)

[26] https://m.youtube.com/watch?v=JG-EX64HBEo (accessed November 2019)

[27] Log into twitter to see the original source: https://twitter.com/DalaiLama/status/332790603966476288 (accessed November 2019)

[28] https://dictionary.cambridge.org/dictionary/english/mindset

[29] This is drawn from the cycle of bereavement created by Elizabeth Kübler-Ross.

Otto Scharmer and Katrin Kaufer (2013); *Leading from the Emerging Future*, 1st edn., Better-Koehler Books, USA,

[30] https://www.edx.org/course/ulab-leading-from-the-emerging-future (accessed November 2019)

[31] See Effectiveness of Solutions-Focused Brief Therapy: A Systematic Qualitative Review of Controlled Outcome Studies. See https://journals.sagepub.com/doi/abs/10.1177/1049731512470859 for one example (accessed November 2019).

[32] Torgheh M, Aliakbari dehkordi M, Alipour A. Effect of humour on burnout and resiliency of nurses . J Holist Nurs Midwifery. 2015; 25 (2) :57-64 http://hnmj.gums.ac.ir/article-1-460-en.html (accessed November 2019)

[33] https://www.mind.org.uk/information-support/drugs-and-treatments/cognitive-behavioural-therapy-cbt/#.Xa9QBC2ZPUo (accessed November 2019)

[34] Therapists might also want to read: O'Hanlon, Bill & Beadle, Sandy (1996) *A Field Guide to Possibility Land*, BT Press.

[35] I understand that some forms of Reality Thinking form part of CBT counselling (Cognitive Behavioural Therapy). You'll find longer more detailed and more developed versions of this at thework.com.

[36] Thanks to Nanette Greenblatt and Kyle Blamer for helping me learn these lessons.

[37] Therapists might also want to read: O'Hanlon, Bill & Beadle, Sandy (1996) *A Field Guide to Possibility Land,* BT Press.

[38] Shared by my peer facilitator, Shaun Lincoln.

[39] https://www.edx.org/course/ulab-leading-from-the-emerging-future

[40] Otto Scharmer and Katrin Kaufer; *Leading from the Emerging Future,* Better-Koehler Books, USA, first edition (2013)

[41] Kyle Balmer (https://bstreetdigital.com) and Anny Johnson (http://officiallyanny.com)

[42] Recap workshop on 'Stretch, Encourage and Change' 2019.

[43] Massive Open Online Course. This one was a mixture of on-line learning, live-streamed sessions, international digital networks and face-to-face group sessions.

[44] www.peoplesfridge.com (accessed November 2019)

[45]Whitmore, J. (2009). Coaching for Performance, 4th edn. London: Nicholas Brealey Publishing.

Printed in Great Britain
by Amazon

57921966R00081